BARACK OBAMA

BARACK OBAMA
IT'S HARD TO PINPOINT JUST WHEN AMERICA STARTED VIEWING BARACK OBAMA AS AN IDEALIZED SUPERMAN... MYTHOLOGIZED EVEN AS HE LIVES AND BREATHES.
AFTER ALL, IN WHAT BIZARRO VERSION OF AMERICA DOES THE MAINSTREAM SO QUICKLY AND EFFORTLESSLY LATCH ONTO A POLITICAL FIGURE AS A SUPERHERO, AFTER BEING LET DOWN AGAIN AND AGAIN BY THEM?
THIS SPOKE TO SOMETHING DEEP-- I'M NOT EVEN SURE KENNEDY GOT A BOBBLEHEAD IN HIS DAY.
BUT, IMPROBABLY, IT REALLY HAPPENED.
FASTER THAN A SPEEDING BULLET, A SELF-PROCLAIMED 'SKINNY GUY WITH A FUNNY NAME' ARRIVED AND FLIPPED WASHINGTON ON ITS EAR.
BECAUSE OF THIS, YOU'LL NOW HAVE A DIFFICULT TIME EXPLAINING TO YOUR KIDS HOW EXTRAORDINARY IT WAS THAT A BLACK MAN BECAME THE 44TH PRESIDENT OF THE UNITED STATES.
TO FUTURE GENERATIONS, THIS MINOR TIDBIT WILL NOT SEEM STRANGE AT ALL.
EVERY STORY HAS A BEGINNING BUT, FOR THIS AUTHOR'S TWO CENTS, BARACK OBAMA'S STORY HAS A PRETTY UNUSUAL ONE...

...IT BEGINS WITH THE *HORSESHOE SANDWICH.*
TEXAS TOAST, COVERED WITH CRINKLE CUT FRIES, SMOTHERED IN SPICY CHEESE SAUCE.
IT'S THE MOST *WONDERFUL* AND *HORRIBLE* THING YOU'LL *EVER* PUT IN YOUR MOUTH.
NO ONE EVEN KNOWS WHY IT'S *CALLED* "THE HORSESHOE."
I MEAN, HORSESHOES ARE SUPPOSED TO BE A SYMBOL OF *LUCK*, BUT A STEADY DIET OF THESE WILL ONLY PLUG YOU UP, PUT YOU SIX FEET UNDER, OR *BOTH*.
IN *SPRINGFIELD*, THE CAPITAL OF ILLINOIS --WHERE I LIVE AND WHERE OBAMA SPENT EIGHT OF HIS FORMATIVE YEARS IN THE STATE SENATE-- WE INVENTED THIS UNHOLY DELICACY. WE'RE FAMOUS FOR IT.
ALONG WITH CREATING THE NATION'S FIRST CORN DOG, FIRST DRIVE THRU RESTAURANT, AND FIRST DEEP-FRIED...
HOLY CRAP. UNTIL, OBAMA CAME TO TOWN, I GUESS SPRINGFIELD WAS PRETTY MUCH FAMOUS FOR KEEPING HOSPITALS IN BUSINESS.
I MEAN, *SPRINGFIELD* IS *ALSO* FAMOUS FOR ABRAHAM LINCOLN.
FOR *25* YEARS, THIS *SMALL* TOWN SHAPED HISTORY'S MOST CELEBRATED PRESIDENT.
BUT THAT WAS, LIKE, *200* YEARS AGO, SO ENOUGH ABOUT HIM...
YEAH... *NOM NOM*... I MEAN... *URP*... IT'S NOT LIKE I WAS EVER COVERED IN DELICIOUS CHEESE GRAVY, SO WHAT'S THE *APPEAL*, EXACTLY?
I'M NOT SURE WHAT PEOPLE EVER SAW IN ME.
I KNOW, RIGHT? THAT'S WHAT *I'VE* BEEN SAYING!
...CRIPES, THESE THINGS ARE GOOD. IT'S LIKE MY TASTE BUDS ARE BEING... *EMANCIPATED* OR SOMETHING!

SO, ANYWAY... I SUPPOSE YOU'RE WONDERING WHAT THIS ALL HAS TO DO WITH BARACK OBAMA. YOU KNOW, BESIDES THAT HE MUST HAVE EATEN HIS SHARE OF HORSESHOES WHILE HANGING OUT IN SPRINGFIELD. HEY, THE GUY USED TO CHAIN SMOKE, SO WHAT'S ONE MORE AWFUL HABIT?
ON BEHALF OF THE GREAT STATE OF ILLINOIS, CROSSROADS OF A NATION, LAND OF LINCOLN, LET ME EXPRESS MY DEEP GRATITUDE FOR THE PRIVILEGE OF ADDRESSING THIS CONVENTION.
...WHAT I THINK IT MEANS, IS THAT UNTIL BARACK OBAMA WALKED ON STAGE TO DELIVER THE DEMOCRATIC NATIONAL CONVENTION KEYNOTE SPEECH IN 2004, THE WHOLE OF AMERICAN POLITICS SEEMED ABOUT AS APPETIZING AS A GREASY, STOMACH-CHURNING, HAMBURGER-INDUCED BELLY CRAMP (WITH FRIES ON TOP). BUT WHEN HE TOLD HIS STORY...
TONIGHT IS A PARTICULAR HONOR FOR ME BECAUSE, LET'S FACE IT, MY PRESENCE ON THIS STAGE IS PRETTY UNLIKELY.
MY FATHER WAS A FOREIGN STUDENT, BORN AND RAISED IN A SMALL VILLAGE IN KENYA. HE GREW UP HERDING GOATS, WENT TO SCHOOL IN A TIN-ROOF SHACK...
OBAMA
...HE SEEMED TO SPELL R-E-L-I-E-F FOR A LOT OF PEOPLE FED UP WITH THE JUNK BEING FED TO THEM, WHO WERE HUNGRY FOR SOMETHING BETTER. SUDDENLY, THE NATION HAD FOUND ITS POLITICAL APPETITE AGAIN.
BUT MAYBE I'M GETTING AHEAD OF THINGS. PEOPLE DON'T START WAVING SIGNS AROUND WITH YOUR NAME ON IT OVERNIGHT.
OR NAMING LOGS AFTER YOU!
UMM... YEAH. YOU SAID IT, ABE.

1967. JIM MORRISON SHOCKS AMERICA BY MAKING A SUBTLE DRUG REFERENCE ON THE ED SULLIVAN SHOW. I KNOW... RISKY STUFF.
BUT PERHAPS MORE SHOCKING...
...IS THAT INTERRACIAL MARRIAGES WERE STILL ILLEGAL IN VIRGINIA, AND 16 OTHER STATES, UNTIL A SUPREME COURT RULING IN '67.
IT WAS IN THIS TENSE CLIMATE THAT THE UNTHINKABLE PAIRING OF A SWEET KANSAS GRAD-STUDENT AND A CHARISMATIC, STUDIOUS EX-GOAT HERDER FROM KENYA'S LUO TRIBE OCCURRED IN HAWAII... WAY BACK IN 1959.
LOVE
NECTION
59
ON ONE OF OUR FIRST DATES, HE TRIED TO DANGLE A GUY OVER A CLIFF!
WHAT COULD I DO? HE DROPPED MY FAVORITE PIPE OVER THE EDGE! CAN'T ANYONE TAKE A JOKE?
HAHAHAHA
BARACK HUSSEIN OBAMA II WAS BORN IN 1961. BEFORE HE WAS THREE, HIS DAD LEFT THEM-- FIRST TO HARVARD FOR A MASTERS IN ECONOMICS, THEN BACK TO KENYA FOR GOOD.
WHAT WAS HE LIKE, GRAMPS?
HEH.
YOUR DAD COULD HANDLE JUST ABOUT ANY SITUATION, BAR, AND THAT MADE EVERYBODY LIKE HIM. SURE OF HIMSELF. NOW THERE'S SOMETHING YOU CAN LEARN FROM YOUR DAD...
CONFIDENCE.
THE SECRET TO A MAN'S SUCCESS.

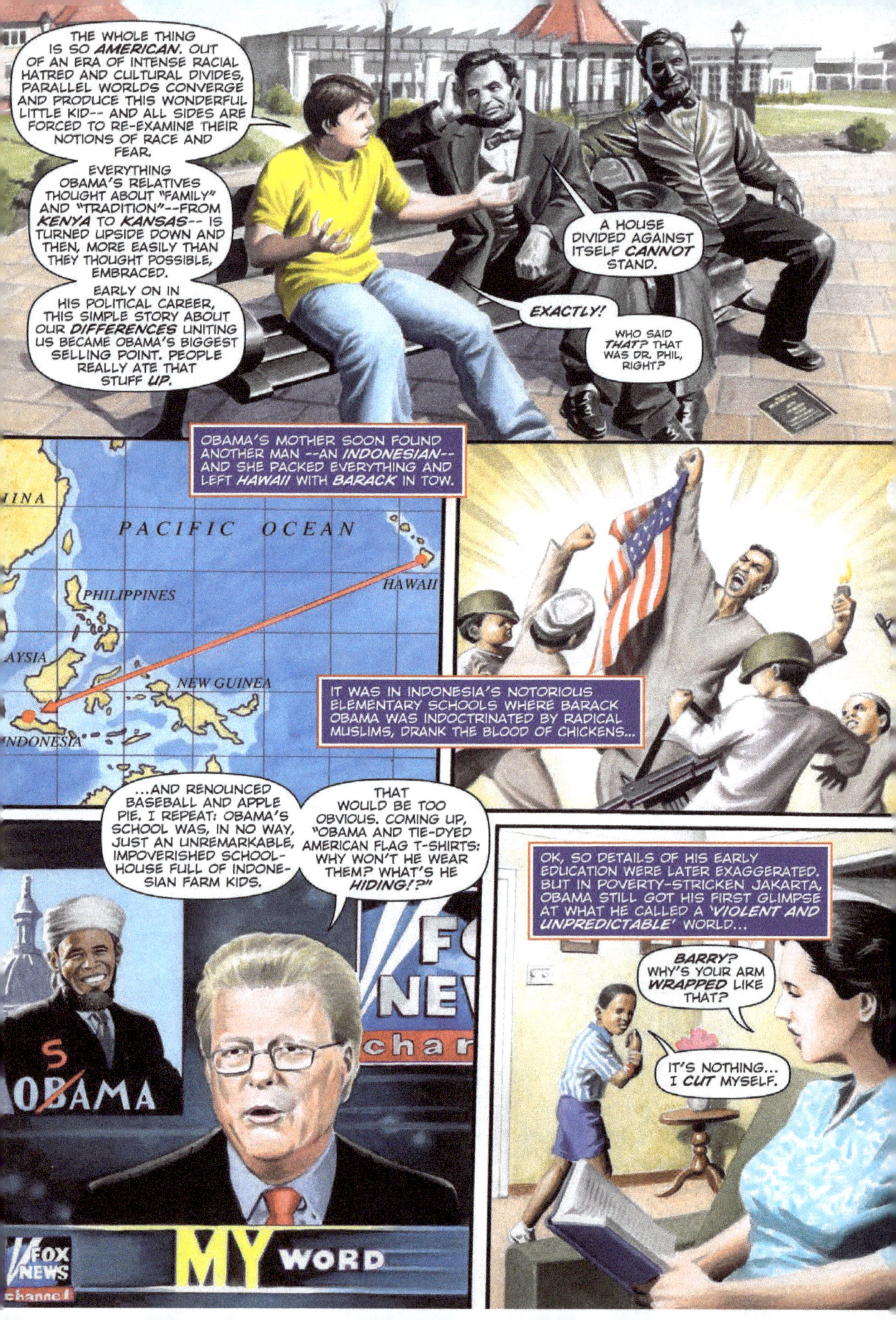

THE WHOLE THING IS SO AMERICAN. OUT OF AN ERA OF INTENSE RACIAL HATRED AND CULTURAL DIVIDES, PARALLEL WORLDS CONVERGE AND PRODUCE THIS WONDERFUL LITTLE KID-- AND ALL SIDES ARE FORCED TO RE-EXAMINE THEIR NOTIONS OF RACE AND FEAR.
EVERYTHING OBAMA'S RELATIVES THOUGHT ABOUT "FAMILY" AND "TRADITION"--FROM KENYA TO KANSAS-- IS TURNED UPSIDE DOWN AND THEN, MORE EASILY THAN THEY THOUGHT POSSIBLE, EMBRACED.
EARLY ON IN HIS POLITICAL CAREER, THIS SIMPLE STORY ABOUT OUR DIFFERENCES UNITING US BECAME OBAMA'S BIGGEST SELLING POINT. PEOPLE REALLY ATE THAT STUFF UP.
A HOUSE DIVIDED AGAINST ITSELF CANNOT STAND.
EXACTLY!
WHO SAID THAT? THAT WAS DR. PHIL, RIGHT?
OBAMA'S MOTHER SOON FOUND ANOTHER MAN --AN INDONESIAN-- AND SHE PACKED EVERYTHING AND LEFT HAWAII WITH BARACK IN TOW.
INA
PACIFIC OCEAN
PHILIPPINES
HAWAII
AYSIA
NEW GUINEA
INDONESIA
IT WAS IN INDONESIA'S NOTORIOUS ELEMENTARY SCHOOLS WHERE BARACK OBAMA WAS INDOCTRINATED BY RADICAL MUSLIMS, DRANK THE BLOOD OF CHICKENS...
...AND RENOUNCED BASEBALL AND APPLE PIE. I REPEAT: OBAMA'S SCHOOL WAS, IN NO WAY, JUST AN UNREMARKABLE, IMPOVERISHED SCHOOL-HOUSE FULL OF INDONE-SIAN FARM KIDS.
THAT WOULD BE TOO OBVIOUS. COMING UP, "OBAMA AND TIE-DYED AMERICAN FLAG T-SHIRTS: WHY WON'T HE WEAR THEM? WHAT'S HE HIDING!?"
S
OBAMA
FOX NEWS channel
MY WORD
OK, SO DETAILS OF HIS EARLY EDUCATION WERE LATER EXAGGERATED. BUT IN POVERTY-STRICKEN JAKARTA, OBAMA STILL GOT HIS FIRST GLIMPSE AT WHAT HE CALLED A 'VIOLENT AND UNPREDICTABLE' WORLD...
BARRY? WHY'S YOUR ARM WRAPPED LIKE THAT?
IT'S NOTHING... I CUT MYSELF.

WE WERE PLAYING, AND...
OH MY GOD!
ST. MARY'S
HELLO? HEY! HELLO?
WHERE ARE ALL THE DOCTORS?
... WE ARE THE DOCTORS.
OBAMA STILL HAS A SCAR FROM THEIR SHODDY STITCHES...

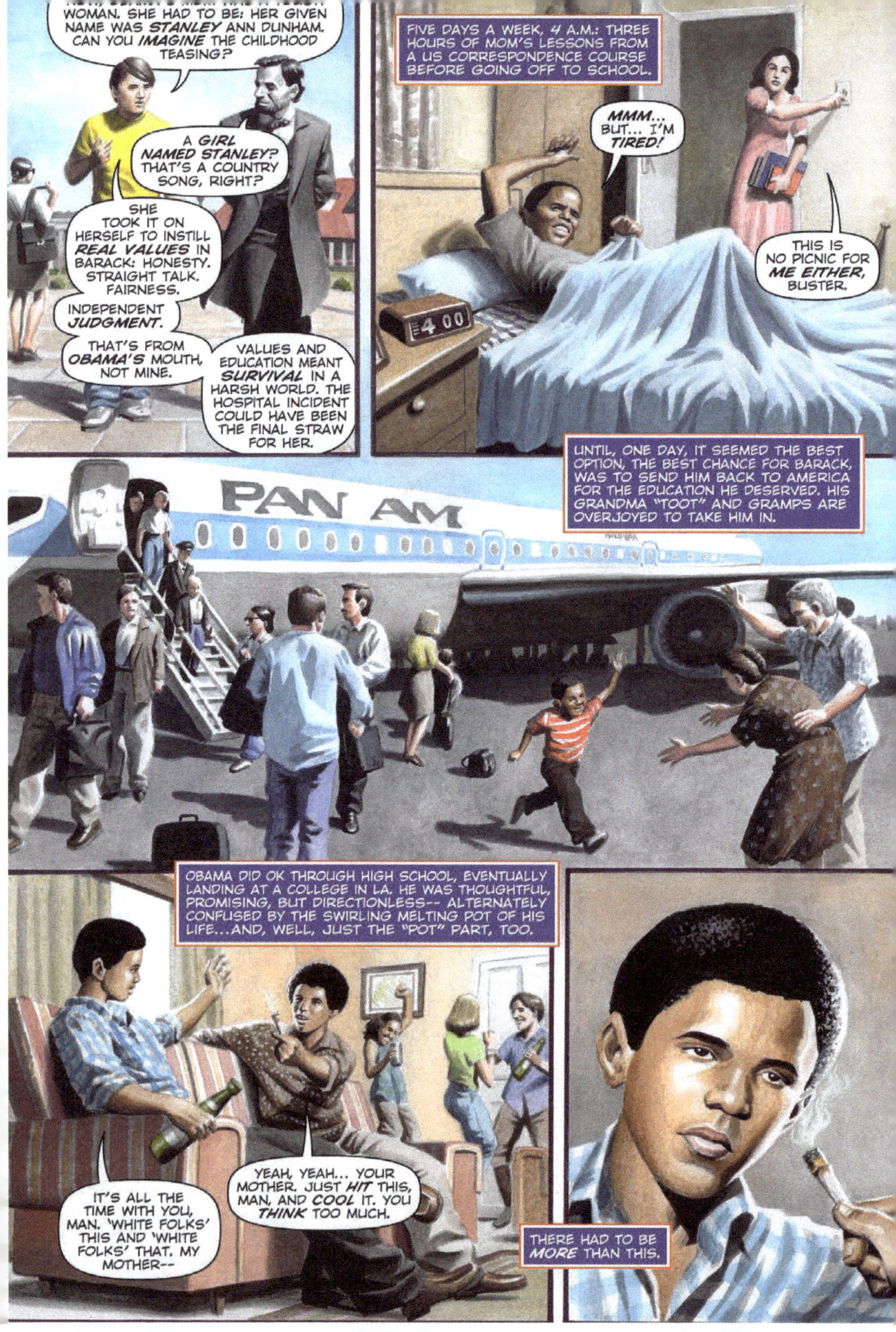
WOMAN. SHE HAD TO BE: HER GIVEN NAME WAS STANLEY ANN DUNHAM. CAN YOU IMAGINE THE CHILDHOOD TEASING?
A GIRL NAMED STANLEY? THAT'S A COUNTRY SONG, RIGHT?
SHE TOOK IT ON HERSELF TO INSTILL REAL VALUES IN BARACK: HONESTY. STRAIGHT TALK. FAIRNESS.
INDEPENDENT JUDGMENT.
THAT'S FROM OBAMA'S MOUTH, NOT MINE.
VALUES AND EDUCATION MEANT SURVIVAL IN A HARSH WORLD. THE HOSPITAL INCIDENT COULD HAVE BEEN THE FINAL STRAW FOR HER.
FIVE DAYS A WEEK, 4 A.M.: THREE HOURS OF MOM'S LESSONS FROM A US CORRESPONDENCE COURSE BEFORE GOING OFF TO SCHOOL.
MMM... BUT... I'M TIRED!
THIS IS NO PICNIC FOR ME EITHER, BUSTER.
4:00
UNTIL, ONE DAY, IT SEEMED THE BEST OPTION, THE BEST CHANCE FOR BARACK, WAS TO SEND HIM BACK TO AMERICA FOR THE EDUCATION HE DESERVED. HIS GRANDMA "TOOT" AND GRAMPS ARE OVERJOYED TO TAKE HIM IN.
PAN AM
OBAMA DID OK THROUGH HIGH SCHOOL, EVENTUALLY LANDING AT A COLLEGE IN LA. HE WAS THOUGHTFUL, PROMISING, BUT DIRECTIONLESS-- ALTERNATELY CONFUSED BY THE SWIRLING MELTING POT OF HIS LIFE...AND, WELL, JUST THE "POT" PART, TOO.
IT'S ALL THE TIME WITH YOU, MAN. 'WHITE FOLKS' THIS AND 'WHITE FOLKS' THAT. MY MOTHER--
YEAH, YEAH... YOUR MOTHER. JUST HIT THIS, MAN, AND COOL IT. YOU THINK TOO MUCH.
THERE HAD TO BE MORE THAN THIS.

A FALSE START IN MANHATTAN AS A BUSINESSMAN. A FEW THANKLESS YEARS WORKING FOR A PUBLIC REFORM OFFICE. A SURPRISE PHONE CALL, AND THE DEATH OF A FATHER HE BARELY KNEW.
GOT ANY CHANGE, PAL? YOU KNOW, REAL CHANGE?
IF HE'D HAVE KNOWN NEW YORK WOULD BE LIKE THIS, HE PROBABLY WOULD HAVE LEFT INSTEAD OF SPENDING HIS FIRST NIGHT THERE IN AN ALLEY. HIS FRIEND FORGOT HE WAS COMING AND LEFT NO APARTMENT KEY. WHOOPS.
1983. CHICAGO. OBAMA IS HIRED TO BECOME A COMMUNITY ORGANIZER ON THE IMPOVERISHED SOUTH SIDE. HE STARTS OVER, DETERMINED THIS TIME TO MAKE A DIFFERENCE IN THIS CORNER OF THE WORLD. HE WAS IDEALISTIC, HEADSTRONG...
...AND HE HAD A LOT TO LEARN ABOUT GETTING PEOPLE INTERESTED IN POLITICS.
Altgeld Gardens: Take Back Your Neighborhood! Meeting at 8
BUT HE KEPT UP HIS "GRASSROOTS" MENTALITY, ORGANIZING THE COMMUNITY PERSON BY PERSON, AND EVENTUALLY...
...PEOPLE STARTED TO LISTEN. MORE IMPORTANTLY, HIS EARLY SUPPORTERS SAY, IS THAT OBAMA LISTENED RIGHT BACK...
...EVEN IF NO ONE COULD GET HIS NAME RIGHT.
OBAMA.
OBAMBA?
OBAMA.
LA BAMBA?
OBAMA.
MADONNA?
SIGH

I GUESS A SMALL TOWN MAYOR IS SORT OF LIKE A COMMUNITY *ORGANIZER*, EXCEPT THAT YOU HAVE ACTUAL RESPONSIBILITIES.
HAHAHAHA
HE PLAYED IT COOL, BUT SARAH PALIN'S FAMOUS DIG, REPEATED AT EVERY CAMPAIGN STOP, HAD TO STING OBAMA. MAYBE IT PROMPTED HIS SLY "LIPSTICK ON A PIG" JOKE. BOTH SIDES GOT THEIR SHOTS IN.
BUT AS AN ORGANIZER, HE TOOK A NEIGHBORHOOD FROM NOTHING TO SECURING A BUDGET OF $400,000 FOR JOB PLACEMENT PROGRAMS AND HOUSING REFORM. AFTER GRADUATING HARVARD AS A TOP LAWYER, THE 30-YEAR-OLD UPSTART MADE GOOD ON HIS PROMISE TO RETURN TO THE SOUTH SIDE AND FOUGHT FOR ECONOMIC DEVELOPMENT AND CIVIL RIGHTS.
HE TURNED DOWN SOME BIG *JOB OFFERS* TO DO IT.
SO I'M NOT SURE HOW YOU'D DEFINE "ACTUAL *RESPONSIBILITIES*," BUT I THINK HE HAD 'EM IN SPADES.
OBAMA'S MASSIVELY ORGANIZED "ILLINOIS PROJECT VOTE" BROUGHT IN *150,000* NEW BLACK VOTERS. ALL IN ALL, AFRICAN AMERICANS TURNED OUT *600,000* STRONG FOR THE *1993* PRESIDENTIAL ELECTION, TURNING ILLINOIS DEMOCRATIC FOR THE FIRST TIME SINCE *1964*, WHEN BARACK WAS THREE.
It's a POWER thing! X
VOTE THRS. NOV. 2
"IT WAS THE MOST EFFICIENT CAMPAIGN I HAVE SEEN IN MY 20 YEARS IN POLITICS."
Chicago Tribune
Clinton Wins!
--SAM BURRELL, ALDERMAN OF THE WEST SIDE'S *29TH* WARD, REGISTRATION DRIVE VETERAN (CHICAGO MAGAZINE, JAN. '93).
AND NOW, IT MADE SENSE TO TRY AND GET MORE DONE...
...BY RUNNING FOR STATE SENATE? IN ILLINOIS? YOU KNOW HOW *DIRTY* ILLINOIS POLITICS ARE, RIGHT? JUST WHAT DO YOU THINK YOU'RE GOING TO ACCOMPLISH?
WELL, I... I GUESS WE'LL SEE.

ILLINOIS POLITICS HAVE... A REPUTATION. THERE'S A REASON OUR MOTTO IS "ILLINOIS: WHERE THE GOVERNORS MAKE THE LICENSE PLATES."
WE'VE HAD SEVEN GOVERNORS INDICTED OR ARRESTED-- AND THOSE WERE JUST THE GUYS STUPID ENOUGH TO GET CAUGHT.
YOU'VE PROBABLY HEARD OF ROD BLAGOJEVICH, WHO ALLEGEDLY TRIED TO SELL OBAMA'S VACANT SENATE SEAT AND GOT IMPEACHED.
OOOO! OOOO! I WANT A COMIC BOOK!
PUT ME IN A COMIC BOOK!
MAKE ONE ABOUT ME!
HERE'S A TRUE STORY. I'M WALKING THROUGH SPRINGFIELD'S ABRAHAM LINCOLN PRESIDENTIAL MUSEUM AND I SPOT A PENNY ON THE GROUND...
I ALMOST WALK RIGHT INTO THIS OLD GUY. I LOOK UP TO APOLOGIZE...
...AND I'M NOSE TO NOSE WITH EX-GOVERNOR GEORGE RYAN: THE GUY NOW IN PRISON FOR A "LICENSES-FOR-BRIBES" SCANDAL. A TRUCK DRIVER WHO OBTAINED ONE OF THESE LICENSES GOT IN A WRECK THAT KILLED SIX LITTLE KIDS, WHICH KICKED OFF THE INVESTIGATION. IT WAS ALL OVER THE NEWS.
AND HERE HE WAS. THIS 75-YEAR-OLD RACKETEER, EXTORTIONIST, ELECTED FELON... JUST STROLLING AROUND IN MY TOWN. STANDING IN LINCOLN'S SHADOW. THE AUDACITY.
TIME AND AGAIN, MEN LIKE GEORGE RYAN SHAPED MY CYNICAL VIEW OF POLITICS.
IN THE STATE SENTATE, OBAMA ONCE WORKED ACROSS PARTY LINES WITH RYAN TO OVERHAUL THE STATE'S DEATH PENALTY SYSTEM, FIGHT PREDATORY HOUSING LENDERS AND GIVE TAX BREAKS TO THE POOR. AND, SOMEHOW, HE AVOIDED THE TEMPTATIONS OF ABUSING POWER AND THE "SMALLNESS OF POLITICS."
THIS DIDN'T MAKE AS MUCH NEWS.

I WANNA HEAR MORE ABOUT THIS "LINCOLN MUSEUM."
BIG SHOCKER. WELL, LET'S SEE... THE LINCOLN MUSEUM CAFE HAS "THEMED TREATS."
YOU CAN ORDER ABRAHAM ICE CREAM, AND EVEN A MARY TODD LINCOLN BROWNIE--
THAT'S A BROWNIE WITH NUTS, BUT IT'S MOSTLY JUST NUTS. SOME WOULD ARGUE, IT'S COMPLETELY NUTS.
IS THAT A JOKE ABOUT MY WIFE?
ABSOLUTELY. ALSO OF NOTE, IS THAT OBAMA SPOKE AT THE DEDICATION CEREMONY, RIGHT ACROSS THE STREET THERE.
HE TAKES ENORMOUS INSPIRATION FROM YOUR LIFE-- QUOTING YOU OFTEN, LOOKING FOR GUIDANCE IN YOUR DECISIONS AND PHILOSOPHY...
APRIL 20, 2005
...LINCOLN ONCE SAID THAT "CHARACTER IS LIKE A TREE AND REPUTATION LIKE ITS SHADOW. THE SHADOW IS WHAT WE THINK OF IT; THE TREE IS THE REAL THING."
AT A TIME WHEN IMAGE ALL TOO OFTEN TRUMPS SUBSTANCE, WHEN OUR POLITICS ALL TOO OFTEN FEEDS, RATHER THAN BRIDGES, DIVISION...
WHEN THE PROSPECTS OF A POOR YOUTH RISING OUT OF POVERTY SEEM OF NO CONSEQUENCE TO THE POWERFUL...
AND WHEN WE EVOKE OUR COMMON GOD TO CONDEMN THOSE WHO DO NOT THINK AS WE DO, RATHER THAN TO SEEK GOD'S MERCY FOR OUR OWN LACK OF UNDERSTANDING...
AT SUCH A TIME IT IS HELPFUL TO REMEMBER THIS MAN WHO WAS THE REAL THING.
LINCOLN REMINDS US THAT OUR ESSENTIAL GREATNESS IS NOT THE SHADOW OF SOPHISTICATION OR POPULARITY, OR WEALTH OR POWER OR FLEETING CELEBRITY.
IT IS THE TREE THAT STANDS IN THE FACE OF OUR DOUBTS AND FEARS AND BIGOTRIES, AND INSISTS WE CAN DO BETTER.
HE STUMBLED ALL OVER HIS WORDS IN THAT SPEECH AND HIS NAME'S SPELLED WRONG ON TV AS "BARAK" --THAT'S KLINGON, I THINK--
BUT HE SEEMED TO BELIEVE THE STUFF HE WAS SAYING ABOUT YOU, OBSESSED WITH "LINCOLN, THE MAN" INSTEAD OF THE "MARBLE GIANT."
WHO TUBE?
THAT OBSERVATION SAYS SOMETHING ABOUT THE WAY OBAMA SEES HIMSELF, I THINK. AN EGO-CHECK. IT'S ALL THERE ON YOU TUBE.

MOST STILL HADN'T HEARD OF OBAMA IN 2004: THOUGH HE HAD WRITTEN TWO BEST-SELLING BOOKS, RAN AND LOST FOR US SENATOR ONCE, EVENTUALLY BECAME A US SENATOR AND SIMPLY STUCK OUT LIKE A SORE THUMB ON THE POLITICAL SCENE.
BARACK OBAMA
The AUDACITY of HOPE
WHAT'S CRAZY IS THAT OBAMA'S EARLY BUZZ GOT AROUND THE SAME WAY THE "KITTEN PLAYING PIANO" DID: VIRAL VIDEO. THIS WAS A FIRST.
WE COACH LITTLE LEAGUE IN THE BLUE STATES, AND, YES, WE'VE GOT SOME GAY FRIENDS IN THE RED STATES... WE ARE ALL ONE PEOPLE...
IN OBAMA'S EVENTUAL ARSENAL OF ARTICULATE, ELOQUENT SPEECHES, THE '04 DNC ADDRESS WOULD BE OBAMA'S 'FREEBIRD'... HE WOVE IT INTO HIS STUMP SPEECHES LATER (AD NAUSEUM, AT TIMES) LIKE A GREATEST HIT TRACK.
THERE IS NOT A LIBERAL AMERICA AND A CONSERVATIVE AMERICA; THERE IS THE UNITED STATES OF AMERICA!
I'M NOT TALKING ABOUT BLIND OPTIMISM HERE, THE ALMOST WILLFUL IGNORANCE THAT THINKS UNEMPLOYMENT WILL GO AWAY IF WE JUST DON'T THINK ABOUT IT, OR THE HEALTH-CARE CRISIS WILL SOLVE ITSELF IF WE JUST IGNORE IT.
THAT'S NOT WHAT I'M TALKING ABOUT. I'M TALKING ABOUT SOMETHING MORE SUBSTANTIAL...
HOPE. HOPE IN THE FACE OF DIFFICULTY, HOPE IN THE FACE OF UNCERTAINTY, THE AUDACITY OF HOPE! IN THE END, THAT IS GOD'S GREATEST GIFT TO US, THE BEDROCK OF THIS NATION, A BELIEF IN THINGS NOT SEEN, A BELIEF THAT THERE ARE BETTER DAYS AHEAD...
"OHIO DISPUTED..."
"TOO CLOSE TO CALL..."
"SWIFT BOAT"
"VOTING CONTROVERSY"
"FLIP FLOP"
"DIEBOLD MACHINES"
"BUSH WINS SECOND TERM"
"BALLOT RE-COUNT"
"FOUR MORE YEARS"
"KERRY CAMP PULLS OUT"
"NO CLEAR WINNER AT THIS HOUR..."
"STATES CONTESTED"
BUT THE 2004 ELECTION WASN'T SOMETHING YOU'D CALL "OPTIMISTIC." THIS WAS DIRTY BUSINESS.

WELL INTO BUSH'S SECOND TERM, HOPE WAS STILL IN SHORT SUPPLY. AND THE ONLY WINDS OF CHANGE...
...WERE DOWN IN NEW ORLEANS. THE GOVERNMENT'S RESPONSE TO HURRICANE KATRINA WAS LACKING. AND NO ONE WAS SHY ABOUT TELLING BUSH THEY'D HAD IT.
GEORGE BUSH DOESN'T CARE ABOUT BLACK PEOPLE.
OH BOY.
SO, IN THIS TIME OF WAR, DESPAIR AND GENERAL CRAPPINESS, OBAMA --LIKE MOST POLITICIANS-- QUICKLY LAID THE GROUNDWORK FOR... WELL, BREAKING HIS FIRST PROMISE, ACTUALLY.
DEC. 30, 2004. ROLLING STONE MAGAZINE.
IT'S NOT GOING TO HAPPEN. I DON'T INTEND TO RUN FOR PRESIDENT IN THE NEXT ELECTION.
...AND THAT IS WHY, IN THE SHADOW OF THE OLD STATE CAPITOL, WHERE LINCOLN ONCE CALLED ON A HOUSE DIVIDED TO STAND TOGETHER, WHERE COMMON HOPES AND COMMON DREAMS STILL LIVE, I STAND BEFORE YOU TODAY TO ANNOUNCE MY CANDIDACY FOR PRESIDENT OF THE UNITED STATES OF AMERICA.
WHOOO!
OBAMA!

FULL DISCLOSURE: I WAS THERE IN THAT INSANE CROWD TO SEE OBAMA. FREEZING MY SCRAWNY BUTT OFF.
WHY WOULD I DO THAT? WHY WOULD I STAND IN BONE-CHILLING WEATHER TO SEE A POLITICIAN?
ALL I COULD REALLY SEE WERE THE TOPS OF HIS BIG EARS, ANYWAY. I'M NOT REALLY A "POLITICAL" GUY.
WHY SHOULD I CARE? WHY NOW? FOR THE FIRST TIME, A LOT OF PEOPLE WERE ASKING THEMSELVES QUESTIONS LIKE THIS. BUT HERE WE WERE, FROM ALL WALKS--
HOPEFUL AND VULNERABLE, ONCE MORE.
BARACK TO THE FUTURE
NOT BLACK ENOUGH, MAN.
TOO BLACK, MAN.
TOO ASIAN. WHAT? HE'S NOT?
OK, TOO BLACK, THEN.
HE'LL NEVER BEAT CLINTON IN THE PRIMARIES. WHY EVEN TRY?
STILL, WE ALL KNEW OBAMA WAS A PIPE DREAM. WE BECAME...
The Fraidy Bunch
WHAT IF HE GETS... YOU KNOW... SHOT?
HEARD HE'S, LIKE, A MUZZ-LIM.
HIS MIDDLE NAME IS "HUSSEIN"? GOOD LUCK, PAL.
HE'S, LIKE, TOO SEXY 2B PREZ. LOL!
OBAMA-GIRL

BUT DESPITE PEOPLE'S DOUBTS AND DISBELIEF, OBAMA'S REAL OBSTACLE COULD BE SUMMED UP IN ONE WORD:
HILLARY.
HEADSTRONG. INTELLIGENT. DETERMINED. CLAWED HER WAY THOUGH THE POLITICAL MUD --AND HER HUSBAND'S MISGIVINGS-- TO BECOME THE FIRST SERIOUS WOMAN CANDIDATE FOR PRESIDENT. NOW THIS WAS GOING TO BE EXCITING.
TO COUNTER, GUYS LIKE DAVID PLOUFFE, HIS CAMPAIGN MANAGER, MIXED OBAMA'S OLD SCHOOL METHODS --GRASSROOTS ORGANIZING-- WITH THE UNTAPPED NEW SCHOOL...
THEY'VE UNDERESTIMATED THE WEB... OUR SMALL ONLINE DONATIONS NUMBER IN THE HUNDREDS OF THOUSANDS, WE'RE MOBILIZING SUPPORTERS NATIONWIDE THROUGH BLOGGING AND TEXT MESSAGES... I'M TELLING YOU, THIS IS HOW WE DO IT.
IT WAS EFFECTIVE. I STILL CAN'T GET OFF THEIR EMAIL CHAIN-- MY FREAKING MOM EMAILS ME LESS THAN DAVID PLOUFFE.
IN THE FIRST REAL TEST --THE 2007 IOWA CAUCUS-- VOTERS SHOCKED PUNDITS BY PICKING OBAMA OVER HILARY CLINTON AND JOHN EDWARDS. THE MAJORITY VOTERS WERE FIRST TIME CACAUSGOERS.
CHANG
CAN BELIEVE I
...I'LL NEVER FORGET THAT MY JOURNEY BEGAN ON THE STREETS OF CHICAGO DOING WHAT SO MANY OF YOU HAVE DONE FOR THIS CAMPAIGN AND ALL THE CAMPAIGNS HERE IN IOWA-- ORGANIZING, AND WORKING, AND FIGHTING TO MAKE PEOPLE'S LIVES JUST A LITTLE BIT BETTER.
...IN THIS ELECTION, WE ARE READY TO BELIEVE AGAIN. THANK YOU, IOWA.
GE
CHRIS IS COOL
THE GUY'S A ROCK STAR! PEOPLE LOVE IT!
AND THE MEDIA WERE EATING IT UP LIKE IT WAS COVERED IN SPICY CHEESE SAUCE.
AMERICANS ARE SKEPTICAL OF THIS "ROCK STAR" BALONEY!
HARDBALL
MSNBC
FOX NEWS channel

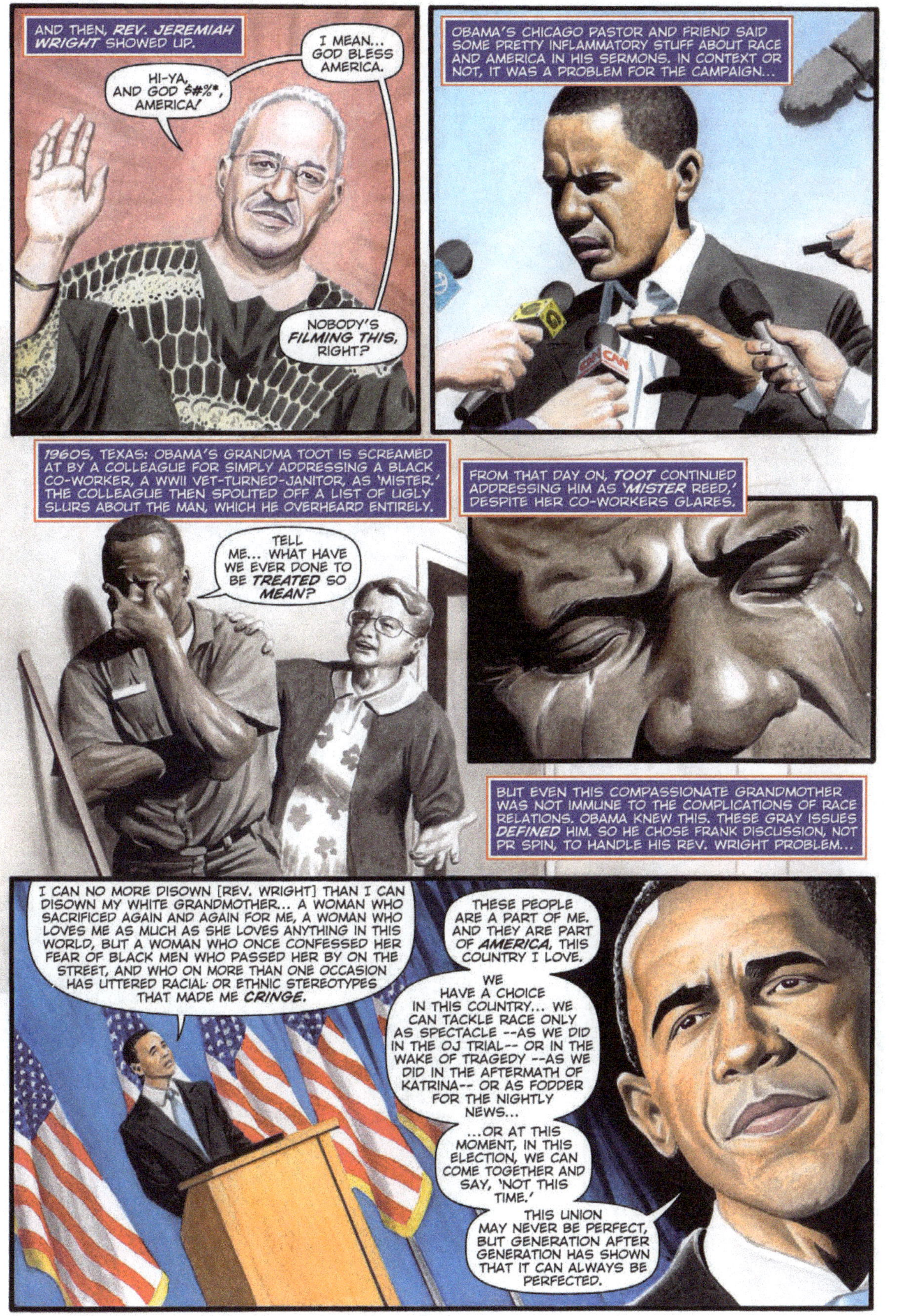

AND THEN, REV. JEREMIAH WRIGHT SHOWED UP.
HI-YA, AND GOD $#%*, AMERICA!
I MEAN... GOD BLESS AMERICA.
NOBODY'S FILMING THIS, RIGHT?
OBAMA'S CHICAGO PASTOR AND FRIEND SAID SOME PRETTY INFLAMMATORY STUFF ABOUT RACE AND AMERICA IN HIS SERMONS. IN CONTEXT OR NOT, IT WAS A PROBLEM FOR THE CAMPAIGN...
CNN
1960S, TEXAS: OBAMA'S GRANDMA TOOT IS SCREAMED AT BY A COLLEAGUE FOR SIMPLY ADDRESSING A BLACK CO-WORKER, A WWII VET-TURNED-JANITOR, AS 'MISTER.' THE COLLEAGUE THEN SPOUTED OFF A LIST OF UGLY SLURS ABOUT THE MAN, WHICH HE OVERHEARD ENTIRELY.
TELL ME... WHAT HAVE WE EVER DONE TO BE TREATED SO MEAN?
FROM THAT DAY ON, TOOT CONTINUED ADDRESSING HIM AS 'MISTER REED,' DESPITE HER CO-WORKERS GLARES.
BUT EVEN THIS COMPASSIONATE GRANDMOTHER WAS NOT IMMUNE TO THE COMPLICATIONS OF RACE RELATIONS. OBAMA KNEW THIS. THESE GRAY ISSUES DEFINED HIM. SO HE CHOSE FRANK DISCUSSION, NOT PR SPIN, TO HANDLE HIS REV. WRIGHT PROBLEM...
I CAN NO MORE DISOWN [REV. WRIGHT] THAN I CAN DISOWN MY WHITE GRANDMOTHER... A WOMAN WHO SACRIFICED AGAIN AND AGAIN FOR ME, A WOMAN WHO LOVES ME AS MUCH AS SHE LOVES ANYTHING IN THIS WORLD, BUT A WOMAN WHO ONCE CONFESSED HER FEAR OF BLACK MEN WHO PASSED HER BY ON THE STREET, AND WHO ON MORE THAN ONE OCCASION HAS UTTERED RACIAL OR ETHNIC STEREOTYPES THAT MADE ME CRINGE.
THESE PEOPLE ARE A PART OF ME. AND THEY ARE PART OF AMERICA, THIS COUNTRY I LOVE.
WE HAVE A CHOICE IN THIS COUNTRY... WE CAN TACKLE RACE ONLY AS SPECTACLE --AS WE DID IN THE OJ TRIAL-- OR IN THE WAKE OF TRAGEDY --AS WE DID IN THE AFTERMATH OF KATRINA-- OR AS FODDER FOR THE NIGHTLY NEWS...
...OR AT THIS MOMENT, IN THIS ELECTION, WE CAN COME TOGETHER AND SAY, 'NOT THIS TIME.'
THIS UNION MAY NEVER BE PERFECT, BUT GENERATION AFTER GENERATION HAS SHOWN THAT IT CAN ALWAYS BE PERFECTED.

THE PRIMARY CONTEST BETWEEN CLINTON AND OBAMA WAGED 10,000 MORE YEARS. WELL... IT SEEMED LIKE IT.
CLINTON WINS!
OBAMA WINS!
CLINTON'S UP!
OBAMA'S DOWN!
THIS JUST IN... REVERSE EVERYTHING WE'VE SAID!
AND EVEN WHEN IT WAS OVER, IT WASN'T OVER.
I'M NOT QUITTING! I'M NOT THROUGH!
I'LL BE READY ON DAY ONE!
HELP ME OBI-WAN KENOBI... YOU'RE MY ONLY HOPE!
WAY TO GO, CHAMP.
THANKS.
HILLARY RAN A TOUGH CAMPAIGN. IF ANYTHING, IT BETTER PREPARED OBAMA FOR THE MONTHS TO COME. IT WAS FAR FROM A CLEAN FIGHT, BUT THAT'S POLITICS. AND YOU HAD TO HAND IT TO HILLARY: SHE WENT OUT SWINGING.
AMBULANCE
PLUS, OPRAH WAS ALREADY BACKING OBAMA, SO IT WAS KIND OF A FOREGONE CONCLUSION.
OPRAH
EVERYONE GETS A CAR!
AND YOU GET A WHITE HOUSE!
SWEETNESS!
AROUND THIS TIME, THINGS GOT REALLY NUTS. I'LL ADMIT SHEPARD FAIRLEY'S ICONIC 'HOPE' POSTER INITIALLY MADE ME UNCOMFORTABLE. IT SUBVERSIVELY BLURS THE LINES BETWEEN PROPAGANDA IMAGERY, CELEBRITY AND POLITICS.
BUT HEY, ART'S SUBJECTIVE. AND IT'S COOL THAT A SKATEBOARDER CREATED THE IMAGE ALL THIS WILL BE REMEMBERED BY. IT'S IN THE SMITHSONIAN NOW. ISN'T THAT INSANE? IT WAS LIKE A NEW GENERATION WAS BEING HEARD FOR THE FIRST TIME.
I THOUGHT PEPSI MADE THOSE DECISIONS.

MEDIA *INFATUATION* WITH OBAMA ACTUALLY REACHED IRRITATING PEAKS...
LIKE WHEN THE BLACK EYED PEAS' WILL.I.AM PUT AN OBAMA SPEECH TO MUSIC? SOOOOO PRETENTIOUS. BUT MOST PEOPLE LIKED IT.
MY HUMPS! WAIT... I MEAN, *"YES WE CAN."*
AND FOR ALL THE ENDLESS PRO-OBAMA HYPE, THERE WAS EQUALLY CRAZY ANTI-OBAMA HYPE...
RIGHT *THERE!* A TERRORIST *FIST JAB!* HOW IS NO ONE ELSE *SEEING THIS?!?*
FOX NEWS channel
THE NON-STOP ELECTION COVERAGE ONSLAUGHT ALMOST MADE ME MISS PRESIDENT BUSH. IT WAS LIKE HE'D DISAPPEARED COMPLETELY...
I'M THE *DECIDER,* BARBIE!
SMOOCHY SMOOCH SMOOCH
WELL... MAYBE I DIDN'T MISS HIM *THAT* MUCH.
BUT THE REPUBLICAN PARTY'S *SALVATION* WAS NEAR...
BANG-O!
MAVERICK

McCAIN'S STORY IS ONE FOR ANOTHER COMIC BOOK, BUT HERE ARE THE BASICS.
WAR HERO AND P.O.W.
CATCH PHRASE: "DRILL, BABY, DRILL!"
73 YEARS YOUNG
WENT FROM DEAD LAST (WITH NO CAMPAIGN MONEY) TO UNDERDOG CHAMPION OF '08 REPUBLICAN PRIMARIES
STRONGLY COMMITTED TO WAR IN IRAQ CURING CAMPAIGN
DRIVES A TRICKED OUT BUS CALLED THE "STRAIGHT TALK EXPRESS"
SAYS "PORK BARREL" A LOT
BUSH SMEAR ADS DERAILED HIS 2000 PRESIDENTIAL BID
...ALSO, HIS "MAVERICK" REPUTATION RUBBED THE REPUBLICAN BASE THE WRONG WAY. HE WAS THE LAST NOMINEE THEY WANTED. BUT, THEN AGAIN, WHO KNOWS WHAT THE GOP WANTED.
EARLY ON, THEIR MESSAGE BOILED DOWN TO "WE'RE NOT GEORGE W. BUSH-- VOTE FOR US."
McCAIN WASTED NO TIME HAMMERING ON OBAMA'S FOREIGN POLICY INEXPERIENCE, TREATING HIM AS NAIVE.
IT WOULD BE A WONDERFUL THING IF WE LIVED IN A WORLD WHERE WE DON'T HAVE ENEMIES. THAT'S NOT THE WORLD WE LIVE IN.
AND UNTIL SEN. OBAMA UNDERSTANDS THAT REALITY, THE AMERICAN PEOPLE HAVE EVERY REASON TO DOUBT WHETHER HE HAS STRENGTH, JUDGMENT AND DETERMINATION TO KEEP US SAFE.
McCAIN
JOHNMcCAIN.C
IT'S TRUE THAT OBAMA HAD DIFFERENT IDEAS ABOUT HOW TO APPROACH FOREIGN RELATIONS.
APRIL, 2007
YOU KNOW THAT OLD BEACH BOYS SONG? "BOMB IRAN?" BOMB, BOMB, BOMB... BOMB, BOMB IRAN...
HEH, HEH...

CLEARLY MEANT TO EVOKE KENNEDY, OBAMA SPOKE TO A CROWD OF 200,000 IN BERLIN, AND THEN MET WITH LEADERS IN IRAQ, AFGHANISTAN, FRANCE AND ENGLAND TO BUMP UP HIS FOREIGN CRED. TO McCAIN'S CHAGRIN, HE WAS A HIT.
JA KÖNNEN WIR!
TRANSLATION: "YES WE CAN!"... I THINK. I DON'T SPEAK GERMAN.
BUT HE STILL HAD PLENTY OF WORK TO DO RIGHT HERE AT HOME, CONVINCING "RED STATES" HE WASN'T AN "ARUGLA EATIN' ELITIST."
...SO IT'S NOT SURPRISING THAT THEY GET BITTER, THEY CLING TO GUNS OR RELIGION OR ANTIPATHY TO PEOPLE WHO AREN'T LIKE THEM.
I LIKE JOHN McCAIN. I REALLY DO. BUT THE CLOSER IT GOT TO ELECTION DAY, THE MORE IT SEEMED LIKE HE WAS GETTING DESPERATE. AND McCAIN'S DESPERATION WORE TWO FACES...
ENTER "HOCKEY MOM" SARAH PALIN, HIS SURPRISE VICE PRESIDENTIAL PICK, AND JOE THE PLUMBER.
IN CASE O
EMERGENC
BREAK GLAS
HI-YA! YOU BETCHA! DARN TOOTIN'! SHUCKY DANG DERN!
WHILE THESE FASCINATING AND STRANGE POLITICAL FIGURES TOOK THE FOCUS OFF OBAMA AS INTENDED, McCAIN NEVER QUITE WRESTLED THE ATTENTION BACK FROM THEM...

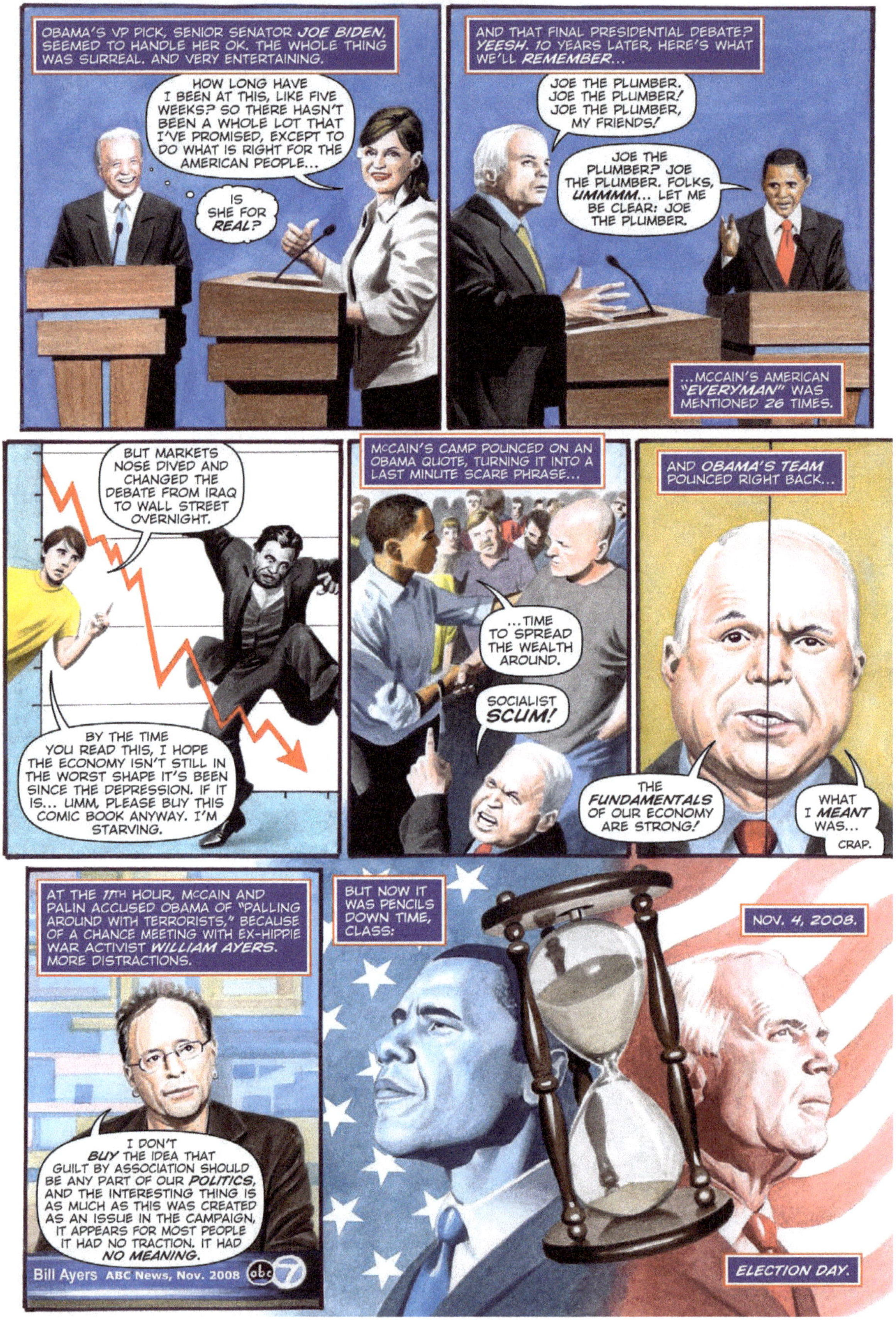

OBAMA'S VP PICK, SENIOR SENATOR JOE BIDEN, SEEMED TO HANDLE HER OK. THE WHOLE THING WAS SURREAL. AND VERY ENTERTAINING.
HOW LONG HAVE I BEEN AT THIS, LIKE FIVE WEEKS? SO THERE HASN'T BEEN A WHOLE LOT THAT I'VE PROMISED, EXCEPT TO DO WHAT IS RIGHT FOR THE AMERICAN PEOPLE...
IS SHE FOR REAL?
AND THAT FINAL PRESIDENTIAL DEBATE? YEESH. 10 YEARS LATER, HERE'S WHAT WE'LL REMEMBER...
JOE THE PLUMBER. JOE THE PLUMBER! JOE THE PLUMBER, MY FRIENDS!
JOE THE PLUMBER? JOE THE PLUMBER. FOLKS, UMMMM... LET ME BE CLEAR: JOE THE PLUMBER.
...MCCAIN'S AMERICAN "EVERYMAN" WAS MENTIONED 26 TIMES.
BUT MARKETS NOSE DIVED AND CHANGED THE DEBATE FROM IRAQ TO WALL STREET OVERNIGHT.
BY THE TIME YOU READ THIS, I HOPE THE ECONOMY ISN'T STILL IN THE WORST SHAPE IT'S BEEN SINCE THE DEPRESSION. IF IT IS... UMM, PLEASE BUY THIS COMIC BOOK ANYWAY. I'M STARVING.
McCAIN'S CAMP POUNCED ON AN OBAMA QUOTE, TURNING IT INTO A LAST MINUTE SCARE PHRASE...
...TIME TO SPREAD THE WEALTH AROUND.
SOCIALIST SCUM!
AND OBAMA'S TEAM POUNCED RIGHT BACK...
THE FUNDAMENTALS OF OUR ECONOMY ARE STRONG!
WHAT I MEANT WAS...
CRAP.
AT THE 11TH HOUR, McCAIN AND PALIN ACCUSED OBAMA OF "PALLING AROUND WITH TERRORISTS," BECAUSE OF A CHANCE MEETING WITH EX-HIPPIE WAR ACTIVIST WILLIAM AYERS. MORE DISTRACTIONS.
I DON'T BUY THE IDEA THAT GUILT BY ASSOCIATION SHOULD BE ANY PART OF OUR POLITICS, AND THE INTERESTING THING IS AS MUCH AS THIS WAS CREATED AS AN ISSUE IN THE CAMPAIGN, IT APPEARS FOR MOST PEOPLE IT HAD NO TRACTION. IT HAD NO MEANING.
Bill Ayers ABC News, Nov. 2008
BUT NOW IT WAS PENCILS DOWN TIME, CLASS:
NOV. 4, 2008.
ELECTION DAY.

THERE WOULD BE NO RE-COUNT, NO HANGING CHADS. "THE AMERICAN PEOPLE HAVE SPOKEN, AND THEY HAVE SPOKEN CLEARLY," McCAIN SAID, GRACIOUSLY, IN HIS CONCESSION SPEECH.
...OBAMA'S GRANDMOTHER TOOT, WHO HELPED SHAPE HER GRANDSON'S UNLIKELY UPBRINGING, CAST HER VOTE BUT WOULDN'T HEAR THE RESULTS. STILL, SHE MUST HAVE KNOWN.
SLAVES WHO BUILT THE WHITE HOUSE OBAMA WOULD ONE DAY TAKE OATH TO SERVE IN... THEY MUST HAVE HOPED.
ANN NIXON COOPER, WHO WOULD TURN 106 BEFORE SHE SAW THIS DAY... SHE MUST HAVE DREAMED...
BARACK'S PARENTS. THEY TOOK THAT INCREDIBLE CHANCE YEARS AGO...
BUT...
JUST ONE DATE. COME ON, WHAT COULD HAPPEN?
HE HAD TO HAVE FELT THE WEIGHT. THE HISTORY. IT MUST HAVE BEEN OVERWHELMING.

FORTY-FOUR AMERICANS HAVE NOW TAKEN THE PRESIDENTIAL OATH. THE WORDS HAVE BEEN SPOKEN DURING RISING TIDES OF PROSPERITY AND THE STILL WATERS OF PEACE. YET, EVERY SO OFTEN THE OATH IS TAKEN AMIDST GATHERING CLOUDS AND RAGING STORMS.
SO IT HAS BEEN. SO IT MUST BE WITH THIS GENERATION OF AMERICANS...
THIS IS THE MEANING OF OUR LIBERTY AND OUR CREED-- WHY MEN AND WOMEN AND CHILDREN OF EVERY RACE AND EVERY FAITH CAN JOIN IN CELEBRATION ACROSS THIS MAGNIFICENT MALL, AND WHY A MAN WHOSE FATHER LESS THAN SIXTY YEARS AGO MIGHT NOT HAVE BEEN SERVED AT A LOCAL RESTAURANT CAN NOW STAND BEFORE YOU TO TAKE A MOST SACRED OATH...
THANK YOU. GOD BLESS YOU. AND GOD BLESS THE UNITED STATES OF AMERICA!
AND LIKE THAT, BARACK OBAMA WAS COMMANDER IN CHIEF. FOR HIS TROUBLE, HE'LL INHERIT TWO WARS, AN ECONOMY IN SHAMBLES, AN ENERGY CRISIS, A CLIMATE EMERGENCY, BILLIONS IN DEBT AND AN IMPENDING WEREWOLF ATTACK.
WEREWOLVES?
BELIEVE IT. PLUS, HE HAS ALL THOSE PROMISES TO MAKE GOOD ON. IT'S A FULL PLATE AND I'M SURE THE OBAMA BACKLASH IS COMING.
HEY, DON'T BLAME ME.
THERE'S ALWAYS A BACKLASH. LIKE NOW... I CAN'T EVEN GET ACROSS TOWN TO GRAB LUNCH BECAUSE HE'S BACK IN SPRINGFIELD TO DELIVER A SPEECH ON LINCOLN. THANKS AGAIN, ABE.
Honest Abe's
HORSESHOE EMPORIUM
24 HOURS
OH, I'M TOTALLY BLAMING YOU.
The End

CONDOLEEZZA
RICE
'09

I WANT YOU TO TELL ME HONESTLY...
DOES THIS LOOK LIKE A Led Zeppelin SUPER-FAN TO YOU?
NOT TO BELITTLE THIS STRONG WOMAN AND HER ACCOMPLISHMENTS... BUT, WHEN YOU THINK OF CONDOLEEZZA RICE, IS SHE BANGING THE DASHBOARD IN TIME TO 'KASHMIR'? AND, IF SO, HOW DOES HER HAIR STAY PERFECT?
AFTER BEING GRILLED BY THE 9/11 COMMISSION, DID SHE RETURN TO HER WATERGATE APARTMENT AND UNWIND TO 'DAZED AND CONFUSED'?
DO THE LYRICS TO 'WHOLE LOTTA LOVE' SECRETLY DRIVE HER WILD?
I'M TELLING YOU, I CAN'T STOP THINKING ABOUT IT: CONDOLEEZZA RICE'S FAVORITE BAND IS LED FREAKING ZEPPELIN.
THIS BLOWS MY MIND.
WHAT DO YOU THINK... IS THERE MORE THAN MEETS THE EYE TO THE FIRST AFRICAN-AMERICAN WOMAN SECRETARY OF STATE?

"...AM I THE ONLY ONE SURPRISED?"
CHANGE IT.
LADIES AND GENTLEMEN, SHE SPENT EIGHT YEARS IN THE BUSH ADMINISTRATION... CONDOLEEZZA RICE!
MARCH 24, 2009
WHAT'S YOUR FAVORITE BAND OF ALL TIME?
LED ZEPPELIN. WHEN I GET ON THE ELLIPTICAL AND EXERCISE, THEN I CAN REALLY BE WITH LED ZEPPELIN. IT'S GREAT.
WAIT...
WHAT?
SURPRISINGLY, TO REALLY UNDERSTAND CONDI, YOU'VE GOTTA START WITH MUSIC.

CON DOCEZZA! CONNN DOCEZZA!
THE STORY GOES THAT CONDI'S MOTHER, AN OPERA FAN, NAMED HER FOR THE ITALIAN MUSICAL NOTATION "CON DOCEZZA"-- OR "WITH SWEETNESS." HER NAME IS UNUSUAL NOW, MORE SO IN 1954.
ALABAMA, 1892
OTHERS POINT TO A MORE HISTORICALLY COMPLEX ORIGIN FOR HER NAME: HER SLAVERY ROOTS.
HER GRANDPARENTS WERE PLANTATION SLAVES, SOME "FAVORED" HOUSE SERVANTS WHO RECEIVED EDUCATION. AN ITALIAN MAN NAMED ALTO-- CONDI'S GREAT-GREAT-GRANDFATHER-- FATHERED CHILDREN WITH THEM.
BUT, FOR SOME REASON, ITALIAN NAMES CONTINUED IN RICE'S LINEAGE FOR GENERATIONS AFTER, DESPITE THE TOUCHY NATURE OF THEIR BIRTHRIGHT.
WE HAVE A RACIAL BIRTH DEFECT THAT WE'VE NEVER QUITE DEALT WITH... WE ARE MORE INTERTWINED AND INTERTANGLED THAN WE WOULD LIKE TO THINK.
IT'S A LEGACY THAT WAS BASICALLY NOT ONE OF CHOICE AND VOLITION BUT OF VIOLENCE AND OPPRESSION... AND SO I THINK THAT'S WHY PEOPLE HAVE TROUBLE ADMITTING IT AND TALKING ABOUT IT AND UNDERSTANDING IT.

THE VULCAN IS ALSO A MAJOR PART OF CONDOLEEZZA'S UPBRINGING.
I DON'T THINK THIS IS LOGICAL-- YOU MUST BE THINKING OF A DIFFERENT VULCAN. PERHAPS THE FAMOUS STATUE IN BIRMINGHAM, ALABAMA, WHERE CONDOLEEZZA WAS BORN?
UMM... RIGHT. SHOULD HAVE RESEARCHED MORE. THANKS, SPOCK.
A PLEASURE TO BE OF ASSISTANCE. NOW, AS THEY SAY, "10-4, GOOD BUDDY."
BIRMINGHAM WAS ONCE KNOWN AS "THE MAGIC CITY," A THRIVING POST-CIVIL WAR STEEL TOWN. THE ROMAN GOD OF FIRE, VULCAN, WATCHED OVER IN THE FORM OF THE WORLD'S LARGEST STEEL SCULPTURE.
CONDI'S GRANDFATHER SETTLED HERE IN 1904 WITH DROVES OF HOPEFUL BLACK WORKERS, LOOKING TO MAKE THEIR WAY AT THE TURN OF THE CENTURY.
SOMEDAY, CONDI'S FOREIGN POLICY TEAM WOULD EVEN BE DUBBED "THE VULCANS" AFTER THE STATUE-- A SYMBOL OF INSPIRATION AND POWER.
BUT BY THE TIME CONDOLEEZZA WAS BORN IN 1954, HER ONCE-STRONG CITY HAD EARNED A NEW NICKNAME...

BIRMINGHAM BECAME "BOMBINGHAM."
BOOOM
NEARLY FIFTY BOMBINGS HAPPENED FROM 1947 TO 1966-- CONDI'S HOMETOWN WAS GROUND ZERO FOR AMERICA'S RACIAL VIOLENCE.
FOR A TIME, CONDOLEEZZA WAS SHELTERED FROM THE VIOLENCE SURROUNDING HER. IN THE UPPER-MIDDLE CLASS SUBURB OF TITUSVILLE, HER DOTING PARENTS SPARED NO EXPENSE FOR THEIR GIRL. BUT INNOCENCE WAS HER REAL LUXURY.
ANGELENA RICE WOULD TEACH HER DAUGHTER PIANO BEFORE SHE COULD READ. CONDI HAD HER FIRST RECITAL AT AGE 4.
DEFIANT IN THE FACE OF SEGREGATION, ANGELENA WENT TO INCREDIBLE LENGTHS TO GIVE HER CHILD OPPORTUNITIES, KNOWING THE DECK WAS STACKED AGAINST THEM: BOTH AS AFRICAN-AMERICANS, AND AS WOMEN.
CONDI'S FATHER-- JOHN, A PASTOR-- WAS A LITTLE EASIER GOING, AND ATTRACTED KIDS TO HIS FELLOWSHIP USING POP MUSIC.
BUT WITHOUT LED ZEPPELIN, OBVIOUSLY.
...AIN'T TO PROUD TO BEG, YOU KNOW IT SWEET DARLIN'...

BUT MOSTLY, HER EDUCATION WAS NON-STOP, STRICT AND STRENUOUS. SHE WOULD LATER SKIP FIRST AND SEVENTH GRADE.
CONDI RECALLS HER YOUTH WARMLY, BUT PERHAPS IT'S TELLING THAT, TO THIS DAY, SHE WON'T READ BOOKS FOR FUN.
WATCH IT, PAL, OR YOU'LL TURN ME OFF OF COMIC BOOKS, TOO!
Physics
CHEMISTRY
AMERICAN HISTORY
THE RICE'S WERE... A TAD OVERPROTECTIVE OF THEIR ONLY CHILD.
GIRLS, WHY DON'T WE SHUT THE GARAGE DOOR TO KEEP THE FLIES OUT.
THAT WOULD BE FINE, MRS. HUNTER... BUT, IN THAT CASE, I'LL HAVE TO GO HOME BECAUSE MOTHER WON'T BE ABLE TO KEEP AN EYE ON ME.
STILL HERE, MOTHER!
BALLET, FIGURE SKATING, MUSIC, ETIQUETTE... IT'S LIKE THEY WANTED HER TO WIN THE LITTLE MISS SUNSHINE PAGEANT.
10
10
10
PERHAPS THAT'S A MISCONCEPTION, THOUGH. IF YOU LOOK DEEPER, IT'S ABOUT CONTROL, CONDI ONCE SAID.
"YOUR OUTWARD IMAGE IS CRITICAL TO REMINDING PEOPLE THAT YOU STILL HAVE CONTROL. THEY'RE NOT DIMINISHING YOUR HUMANITY."

1961
BURGER-PHILLIPS CO.
AS BLACK AMERICANS IN BIRMINGHAM, CONTROL WASN'T EASY TO MAINTAIN FROM THOSE WHO SOUGHT TO CONSTANTLY STRIP IT AWAY.
IMAGINE THIS: WHEN SHOPPING IN THOSE DAYS, BLACKS HAD TO WEAR SKULLCAPS TO TRY ON HATS FOR FEAR THEIR HEADS MIGHT TOUCH THE SAME HAT AS A WHITE CUSTOMER.
OH DEAR...
SHE IS NOT TO TOUCH THE MERCHANDISE.
LEARN TO CONTROL HER, AND...
GET YOUR MINIMUM-WAGE MITTS AWAY FROM MY CHILD. DO YOU KNOW HOW MUCH MONEY I'VE SPENT HERE? SHE'LL TOUCH EVERY HAT IN THE STORE IF SHE WANTS.
CONDOLEEZZA ... GO TOUCH THIS WOMAN'S HATS.
TOUCH.
TOUCH.
TOUCH.
TOUCH.

"THE YEAR 1963 IN BIRMINGHAM SHATTERED CONDOLEEZZA RICE'S COMFORTABLE COCOON." -ELISABETH BUMILLER, BIOGRAPHER
JOCKEY BOY RESTAURANT
101
THE KU KLUX KLAN, BOMBINGS, BLOODSHED-- IT SEEMS STRANGE TO THINK SOME BLACKS DID NOT WANT A PREACHER NAMED MARTIN LUTHER KING COMING TO BIRMINGHAM TO PROTEST.
MIDDLE-CLASS BLACKS LIKE THE RICE'S WERE SEGREGATED, BUT ADMITTEDLY COMFORTABLE. ONCE KING ROCKED THE BOAT, THERE WOULD BE NO GOING BACK. THEY KNEW THE COST.
SOME OF THE PEOPLE SITTING HERE TODAY WILL NOT COME BACK ALIVE FROM THIS CAMPAIGN.
BAN RACISM FOREVER
STOP RACISM
WE SHALL OVERCOME
KNOWING WHAT HE KNEW ABOUT MAN'S CAPACITY TO HATE, KING CONTROVERSIALLY CALLED BIRMINGHAM'S CHILDREN TO RALLY AND MARCH.
AT 100 FEET, THEIR HOSES COULD KNOCK BRICKS LOOSE FROM A WALL.
BUT AT POINT BLANK RANGE... THE EFFECT IS TOO AWFUL TO IMAGINE.

CONDI'S FATHER RELUCTANTLY JOINED A NEIGHBORHOOD PATROL TO PROTECT HIS FAMILY. THERE WAS NO REST.
FROM THIS DAY ON, CONDOLEEZZA'S LIFE WOULD BE PLAGUED BY ACTS OF TERRORISM.
SEPT. 15, 1963 SIXTEENTH STREET BAPTIST CHURCH
KING AND HIS FOLLOWERS OVERCAME: ALABAMA'S SCHOOLS WERE DESEGREGATED. AND THEN, ON A QUIET SUNDAY MORNING...
ONE WAY
HOLD ON, I FEEL SOMETHING.
OH MY GOD... OH GOD...

AMONG THE BOMBING VICTIMS, 4 GIRLS. INCLUDING CONDOLEEZZA'S FRIEND, DENISE MCNAIR.
OH LORD... PLEASE...
2005
WHENEVER I THINK OF ADDIE AND DENISE AND CAROLE AND CYNTHIA, I THINK, TOO, OF WHAT OCCURRED THERE AND WHAT THEY REPRESENT.
WHICH IS THAT WHEN AMERICA EXPERIENCED ITS OWN HOMEGROWN TERRORISM, IT WAS MEANT TO SHATTER OUR SPIRIT.
IN 1966, TWO YEARS AFTER PRESIDENT JOHNSON HAD SIGNED THE CIVIL RIGHTS ACT, CONDI AND FAMILY WOULD MOVE. PARTLY BECAUSE OF HER FATHER'S NEW TEACHING JOB... PARTLY TO ESCAPE THE SOUTH.
H-B9F2
RAMBLE ON! SING MY SONG!
RICE GRADUATED HIGH SCHOOL AT ONLY 15 IN 1970-- AROUND THE TIME LED ZEPPELIN ARRIVED. WHAT WAS LEFT TO ACCOMPLISH?
SO BORED... WONDER HOW THIS RECORD SOUNDS BACKWARDS?
...CONDO-LEEZ-AH... BECOME A... PROFESSIONAL MUSICIAN... LIKE... USSSS... RRRAMGRAMG... DEVILS... FOOD... CAAAKE...
UHHH...
OKAY, OKAY...SO MAYBE CONDI DIDN'T HEAR SECRET, BACKWARDS MESSAGES IN A LED ZEPPELIN RECORD. BUT SOMETHING LED HER TO PURSUE A CAREER OF PROFESSIONAL MUSIC IN COLLEGE.

THE PROBLEM IS, THOUGH CONDI WAS A GOOD PIANO PLAYER, MANY YOUNGER STUDENTS COULD PLAY IN MINUTES WHAT IT TOOK HER YEARS TO LEARN. SHE HAD AN EPIPHANY: "CONCERT PIANIST" WAS NOT A FEASIBLE CAREER.
WOW.
THE DREAM SHE'D HAD SINCE AGE THREE WAS SUDDENLY SHATTERED. AND SHE'D NEVER SETTLE FOR JUST TEACHING PIANO.
AND SINCE THEY'D ALREADY BOUGHT HER A $13,000 GRAND PIANO, CONDI'S PARENTS WERE VERY ILL-PLEASED WITH HER CHANGE OF HEART.
WHAT ARE YOU GOING TO DO WITH YOUR LIFE THEN? WAITRESS?
I'D RATHER WAITRESS THAN TEACH PIANO! AND SO WHAT IF I DO? IT'S MY LIFE!
WELL, IT'S OUR MONEY. PICK A NEW CAREER. AND QUICK.
NOT TO BE FLIPPANT, BUT CONDOLEEZZA FELL INTO INTERNATIONAL POLITICS THE WAY PEOPLE PICK BINGO NUMBERS-- TOTALLY BY CHANCE.
WHEEL OF CAREERS
CATTLE RUSTLER
LITERARY AGENT
FITNESS TRAINER
DENTAL HYGENIST
AUTO REPAIR
BEAVER TRAPPER
INTERNATIONAL POLITICS
UMPIRE
INVENT THE INTERNET
BASIC CABLE CLIP SHOW HOST
HIGH SCHOOL TEACHER
SECRETARY OF STATE
BUT THE RIGHT PERSON, THE RIGHT TEACHER, CAN SHAPE YOUR ENTIRE LIFE. AND SO IT WAS FOR CONDOLEEZZA, AND HER MENTOR, JOSEF KORBEL.
A RESPECTED AND INFLUENTIAL EXPERT ON SOVIET POLITICS, KORBEL COINCIDENTALLY WAS ALSO FATHER TO MADELEINE ALBRIGHT, THE FUTURE FIRST WOMAN SECRETARY OF STATE.

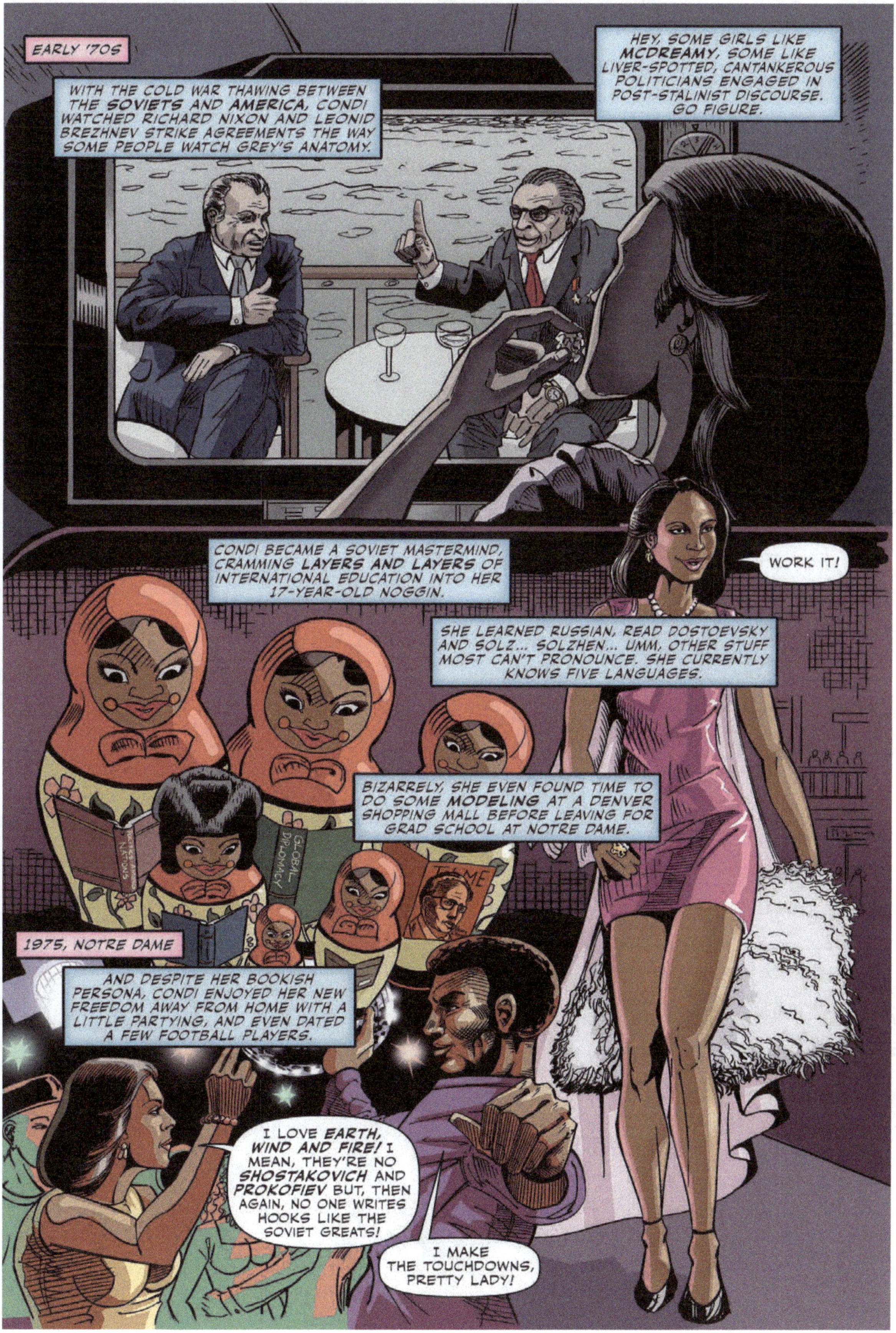
EARLY '70S
WITH THE COLD WAR THAWING BETWEEN THE SOVIETS AND AMERICA, CONDI WATCHED RICHARD NIXON AND LEONID BREZHNEV STRIKE AGREEMENTS THE WAY SOME PEOPLE WATCH GREY'S ANATOMY.
HEY, SOME GIRLS LIKE MCDREAMY, SOME LIKE LIVER-SPOTTED, CANTANKEROUS POLITICIANS ENGAGED IN POST-STALINIST DISCOURSE. GO FIGURE.
CONDI BECAME A SOVIET MASTERMIND, CRAMMING LAYERS AND LAYERS OF INTERNATIONAL EDUCATION INTO HER 17-YEAR-OLD NOGGIN.
WORK IT!
SHE LEARNED RUSSIAN, READ DOSTOEVSKY AND SOLZ... SOLZHEN... UMM, OTHER STUFF MOST CAN'T PRONOUNCE. SHE CURRENTLY KNOWS FIVE LANGUAGES.
BIZARRELY, SHE EVEN FOUND TIME TO DO SOME MODELING AT A DENVER SHOPPING MALL BEFORE LEAVING FOR GRAD SCHOOL AT NOTRE DAME.
GLOBAL DIPLOMACY
TIME
1975, NOTRE DAME
AND DESPITE HER BOOKISH PERSONA, CONDI ENJOYED HER NEW FREEDOM AWAY FROM HOME WITH A LITTLE PARTYING, AND EVEN DATED A FEW FOOTBALL PLAYERS.
I LOVE EARTH, WIND AND FIRE! I MEAN, THEY'RE NO SHOSTAKOVICH AND PROKOFIEV BUT, THEN AGAIN, NO ONE WRITES HOOKS LIKE THE SOVIET GREATS!
I MAKE THE TOUCHDOWNS, PRETTY LADY!

A QUICK WORD IS IN ORDER ABOUT CONDOLEEZZA'S POLITICAL AFFILIATIONS. I KNOW, I KNOW... *YAWN*. STICK WITH ME HERE, FOLKS.
CONDI VOLUNTEERED FOR DEMOCRAT GARY HART'S CAMPAIGN IN 1980, BUT THEN VOTED FOR REPUBLICAN SUPERSTAR RONALD REAGAN IN THE NEXT PRESIDENTIAL ELECTION. REAGAN'S DEMOCRATIC OPPONENT, JIMMY CARTER, MAY HAVE BEEN A FELLOW SOUTHERNER, BUT SHE HAD PROBLEMS WITH THE WAY HE WOULD HANDLE THE SOVIETS.
THE OTHER REASON FOR CONDI'S REPUBLICAN ALLEGIANCE? IN 1952, CONDI'S FATHER TRIED TO VOTE DEMOCRATIC AND WAS SUBJECTED TO A BOGUS "POLL TEST," AND TOLD IF HE FAILED THE TEST, HE COULDN'T VOTE.
THIS WAS AN ACTUAL METHOD USED TO KEEP BLACKS OUT OF VOTING BOOTHS. I *SWEAR* IT'S TRUE.
RICE, JOHN. HERE TO REGISTER AS A DEMOCRA--
NOT SO FAST. FIRST YOU GOTTA GUESS HOW MANY JELLY BEANS ARE IN THIS JAR.
...
AWW, C'MON... CAN'T I JUST *HAVE* ONE?
REPUBLIC PARTY
OH GEE MISTER, COME RIGHT IN, COME RIGHT IN!
WELCOME TO THE REPUBLICAN PARTY! CAN I GET YOU *ANYTHING?* HAVE YOU EATEN? WE HAVE LOTS OF JELLY BEANS, MAN THEY'RE *GOOD!*
BUT, ACROSS TOWN, THE *REPUBLICANS* WERE LOSING MEMBERS AND TAKING *ANYBODY* IN. JOHN RICE WAS A LOYAL REPUBLICAN FROM THAT DAY ON AND, EVENTUALLY, HIS DAUGHTER FOLLOWED SUIT.
1981
AFTER CONDI'S TEACHER, JOSEF KORBEL PASSED AWAY, SHE WAS CRUSHED. BUT SHE VOWED TO MAKE HIM PROUD, AND CONTINUED HER EDUCATION WITH AN EYE TOWARDS MILITARY INTELLIGENCE, WHICH NOW FASCINATED HER.
MADE UP MY MIND TO MAKE A NEW START, GOING TO CALIFORNIA WITH AN ACHING IN MY HEART...
AND SHE WOULD DO IT FROM THE PRESTIGIOUS STANFORD UNIVERSITY.

WITH RONALD REAGAN AS COMMANDER-IN-CHIEF, CONDOLEEZZA'S GROWING INTERNATIONAL EXPERTISE SEEMED MORE RELEVANT THAN EVER--
A HOSTAGE CRISIS WITH IRAN, A SOVIET-CUBAN MILITARY BUILD-UP IN GRENADA, THE COLD WAR ESCALATING WITH RUSSIA...
PIZZAZZ!
PLUS, WITH LIBERACE ON TOP OF HIS GAME, IT WAS GONNA BE EXTRA HARD TO GO BACK TO BEING A CONCERT PIANIST.
DRIVEN TO SUCCEED IN A MALE-DOMINATED FIELD, CONDI STUDIED HARD AT THE STANFORD LINEAR ACCELERATOR CENTER, WHERE SHE LEARNED THE PHYSICS BEHIND NUCLEAR WEAPONS.
...AND THEN THAT THING CONNECTS WITH THAT THING AND EVERYTHING GOES 'BOOM'. *
I SEE. I SEE.
*[EDITOR'S NOTE: NUCLEAR PROCESS SIMPLIFIED DUE TO SPACE LIMITATIONS]
BEFORE LONG, SHE WAS TEACHING AT STANFORD FULL TIME, GIVING SPEECHES AND WRITING POLITICAL SCIENCE BOOKS ABOUT THE SOVIET UNION.
BUT THEN, MORE DEVASTATING NEWS.
I JUST WANT YOU TO KNOW, WE'RE ON OUR WAY TO THE HOSPITAL...
HER MOTHER-- THE MOST OUTSPOKEN, SUPPORTIVE AND LOVING WOMAN IN CONDI'S LIFE-- HAD SUCCUMBED TO CANCER.
ANGELENA TAUGHT CONDI SHE MUST BE "TWICE AS GOOD" TO GET AHEAD IN AN UNFAIR WORLD.
SHE ALSO TAUGHT HER, IN AMERICA-- WHETHER AS A PIANIST OR A POLITICIAN-- SHE COULD WEAR ANY HAT SHE PLEASED. NO MATTER WHAT ANYONE SAID.

MEET THE BUSHES!
President George HW Bush
First Lady Barbara Bush
Future President George W. Bush
Millie, First Dog
CONDI'S LIFE WOULD CHANGE FOREVER IN 1988, AFTER MEETING A NICE TEXAS FAMILY.
SHE TELLS ME EVERYTHING I KNOW ABOUT THE SOVIET UNION.
PLUS, I'VE SEEN "ROCKY 4" EIGHT TIMES.
AT STANFORD, CONDI CAUGHT THE EYE OF THE PRESIDENT, AND BECAME HIS NATIONAL SECURITY ADVISOR-- AN ENORMOUS RESPONSIBILITY.
THOUGH YOUNG, CONDI QUICKLY GAINED A REPUTATION FOR BEING DIPLOMATIC, INTELLIGENT... AND TOUGH AS NAILS.
WE'RE HERE, MR. YELTSIN. FOR SECURITY REASONS, WE'LL ENTER THE WHITE HOUSE THROUGH THE BACK...
A SERVICE ENTRANCE?! DO YOU KNOW WHO I AM? I'M NOT GETTING OUT OF THE CAR FOR THIS.
...LIKE WHEN SHE LITERALLY DRUG A STUBBORN BORIS YELTSIN UP A FLIGHT OF STAIRS, IRONICALLY, INTO A DIPLOMACY MEETING.
YOU KNOW... FOR THE GREATER GOOD.
RIGHT THIS WAY, SIR. I INSIST.
RICE'S HARD WORK WAS AN IMPORTANT PART OF THE REUNIFICATION OF SOCIALIST EAST AND DEMOCRATIC WEST GERMANY AS ONE FREE COUNTRY.
NOT TO MENTION, MAKING SURE THE SOVIETS DIDN'T FEEL THREATENED, LOSE THEIR COOL AND LAUNCH NUCLEAR WARHEADS.
BUT AS THE COLD WAR WAS ENDING...
1991
...ANOTHER WAR WAS BEGINNING.
BUT IRAQ WOULDN'T BE CONDI'S HEADACHE. NOT YET, ANYWAY.
SHE WAS HEADED BACK TO STANFORD TO TEACH AGAIN, AND WOULD EVEN BECOME PROVOST OF THE ENTIRE SCHOOL-- THE FIRST BLACK WOMAN, AND YOUNGEST PERSON, TO EVER DO SO.

CONDI, BY SOME ACCOUNTS, HAD CHANGED: SHE WAS TOUGHER, MORE SELF-CONFIDENT AND VERY CONSERVATIVE-MINDED.
WELFARE RECIPIENTS TAKE ADVANTAGE OF THE GOVERNMENT... WHY CAN'T THEY JUST PULL THEMSELVES UP BY THEIR BOOTSTRAPS?
THEY... WELL, THEY CAN'T AFFORD BOOTS.
CONDI WAS SUDDENLY IN DEMAND BY SEVERAL CORPORATIONS BECAUSE OF HER FOREIGN RESUME, WHERE SHE MADE HUNDREDS OF THOUSANDS ADVISING AND ASSISTING COMPANIES ON INTERNATIONAL DEALS.
CHEVRON EVEN NAMED AN OIL TANKER AFTER HER IN 1993.
SS Condoleezza Rice
GEORGE W. BUSH WOULD SOON COME CALLING, BASED ON HER SUCCESS IN HIS DAD'S ADMINISTRATION AND HIS PERCEPTION THAT HER EXPERIENCE "WAS LIKE THAT OF AN ATTENTIVE PERSON."
SHE'S REALLY SMART!*
[*ACTUAL QUOTE]
AMONG OTHER THINGS, THIS WOULD LEAD TO CONDI'S TANKER BEING RE-NAMED DUE TO PUBLIC FUROR OVER GEORGE W. BUSH'S TIES TO OIL.
zza Rice
BEFORE BECOMING PRESIDENT, BUSH HADN'T GOTTEN OUT MUCH. CONDI HAD QUITE A JOB AHEAD OF HER IN SCHOOLING BUSH ON WORLD AFFAIRS AND LEADERS.
OVER IN PAKISTAN, YOU'VE GOT... PEREZ... PERVEZ MOOSHAR... OH, YOU KNOW HIS NAME. FUNNY LOOKIN' DUDE. HELP ME OUT HERE, CONDI.
TRAGICALLY, NINE DAYS BEFORE SHE JOINED THE ADMINISTRATION, CONDI'S FATHER PASSED AWAY.
THAT'S THE TIME WHEN SHE REALLY TOOK TO BUSH-- THE TWO HAD UNUSUAL CHEMISTRY AND RELIANCE ON EACH OTHER. IN A WAY, THIS WAS HER FAMILY NOW.
HER LOYALTY TO BUSH WAS NO DIFFERENT THAN IT HAD BEEN WITH OTHER OLDER MEN IN HER LIFE-- FROM MENTORS TO PROFESSORS. TO A FAULT, SOME SAID.
BY SEPTEMBER, THEIR LIVES WOULD BE FOREVER INTERCONNECTED.

SEPT. 11, 2001
"THE PENTAGON'S BEEN HIT..."
"GET THE PRESIDENT ON THE PHONE"
DID WE ENGAGE A CIVILIAN AIRCRAFT IN PENNSYLVANIA!?! ANSWER ME!
"THERE'S NO CELL PHONE SERVICE..."
"ARE WE SURE IT WAS TERRORISTS?"
"THE SECOND WORLD TRADE CENTER TOWER JUST HAD ANOTHER EXPLOSION... IT IS COLLAPSING... WE PAUSE TO LET YOU ABSORB THIS PICTURE. A CATASTROPHE ON THE TIP OF MANHATTAN. THERE ARE NO WORDS THAT CAN DESCRIBE THIS. IT'S A TIME TO WATCH, ABSORB AND THINK..."
HOW DID THIS HAPPEN?
IT'S THE QUESTION ENDLESS BOOKS WOULD BE WRITTEN ABOUT.
ONE FAMILIES WOULD WAKE UP WITH ON THEIR LIPS, FOREVER, FROM THAT DAY FORWARD.
ONE JURIES AND PEERS DELIBERATED OVER, POINTING FINGERS.
A QUESTION CONDOLEEZZA WOULD HAVE TO ANSWER FOR THE REST OF HER LIFE.
SEPT. 11, 2001. 11 PM
"DAZED AND CONFUSED."
"COMMUNICATION BREAKDOWN."
NOW THERE ARE TWO LED ZEPPELIN SONGS THAT MUST HAVE BEEN IN HEAVY ROTATION ON CONDI'S IPOD FOLLOWING 9/11.
WE'LL HAVE TO GO TO THE BUNKER FOR THE NIGHT, SIR.
IT COULD BE A FALSE ALARM, BUT THERE HAVE BEEN MORE THREATS OF--
WHOA, WHOA. YOU WANT ME TO SLEEP...
TO MANY HISTORIANS, THESE CONCEPTS WOULD DEFINE THE BUSH ADMINISTRATION'S REACTION TO THE WORST ATTACK ON AMERICAN SOIL.
...ON THAT? I'M NOT STAYING HERE. IF THE TERRORISTS WANT TO FIND ME, THEY'LL FIND ME IN THE OVAL OFFICE.
CONDI, YOU COMING?
ABSOLUTELY, MR. PRESIDENT.

AT FIRST, CONDI THOUGHT 9/11 WOULD PUT SITUATIONS IN IRAQ WITH SADDAM HUSSEIN ON THE BACKBURNER. AFTER ALL, IT WAS OSAMA BIN LADEN THEY WERE AFTER.
WASN'T IT?
"AXIS OF EVIL."
THE PRESSURE ON THE ADMINISTRATION WAS ENORMOUS, AND EVERYONE WANTED INFLUENCE OVER GEORGE BUSH'S NEXT MOVE.
YOU'RE GOING TO BE THE PROUD OWNER OF 25 MILLION PEOPLE... THEIR HOPES, ASPIRATIONS AND PROBLEMS. YOU'LL OWN IT ALL.
SOME WANTED REVENGE AND QUICK ACTION. OTHERS, WHO HAD EXPERIENCED WAR, WERE MORE CAUTIOUS. NO ONE SEEMED TO BE ON THE SAME PAGE.
THE US HAD TO RESPOND, THOUGH.
BUT HOW?
"I'VE ASKED MYSELF A THOUSAND TIMES WHAT MORE WE COULD HAVE DONE," CONDI WOULD LATER TELL THE 9/11 COMMISSION INVESTIGATORS. "I KNOW THAT HAD WE THOUGHT THAT THERE WAS AN ATTACK COMING IN WASHINGTON OR NEW YORK, WE WOULD HAVE MOVED HEAVEN AND EARTH TO TRY AND STOP IT."
CLASSIFIED
BIN LADEN DETERMINED TO STRIKE IN US
HOW DID THIS HAPPEN?
16 St
HOW DO YOU STOP THEM?

BUSH RARELY, IF EVER, ASKED CONDI'S OPINION POINT BLANK. AND NOW, THE LEADER OF THE FREE WORLD WOULD ASK HIS TRUSTED FRIEND THE BIGGEST QUESTION SHE WOULD EVER BE POSED.
YOU THINK WE SHOULD DO THIS?
SHE HAD HEARD ALL THE EVIDENCE. CIA DIRECTOR GEORGE TENET CLAIMED WEAPONS OF MASS DESTRUCTION IN IRAQ.
IT'S A SLAM DUNK!
[SPOILER ALERT: NOT A SLAM DUNK.]
SHE FELT HER EARLY DIPLOMATIC, COUNTERTERRORISM MEETINGS WITH COUNTRIES LIKE PAKISTAN HADN'T WORKED.
SO SHE MADE HER DECISION ABOUT SADDAM.
YES.
TO LET THIS THREAT IN THIS PART OF THE WORLD PLAY VOLLEYBALL WITH THE INTERNATIONAL COMMUNITY THIS WAY WILL COME BACK TO HAUNT US SOMEDAY. THAT IS THE REASON TO DO IT.

THE WAR IN IRAQ.
IT'S THE REASON YOU KNOW CONDOLEEZZA RICE'S NAME.
IT'S DEFINITELY THE REASON SOME PEOPLE WON'T GO NEAR THIS COMIC BOOK.
THE TERM "DIVISIVE WAR" IS AN UNDERSTATEMENT.
WHATEVER YOU BELIEVE, HERE ARE SOME FACTS:
THE US DID NOT FIND WEAPONS OF MASS DESTRUCTION IN IRAQ-- THE INTELLIGENCE WAS PROVEN FAULTY.
THE US WAS NOT IMMEDIATELY GREETED AS LIBERATORS, AS DONALD RUMSFELD ONCE PRESUPPOSED.
RCADO
POST-SADDAM IRAQ COLLAPSED INTO CIVIL WAR AND CHAOS, WITH NO EXIT IN SIGHT.
AND BY THE TIME CONDI WAS OFFERED THE SECRETARY OF STATE POSITION IN BUSH'S SECOND TERM, THE TIDE OF PUBLIC OPINION TURNED ON CONDOLEEZZA AND HER BOSS.
WE DON'T WANT THE SMOKING GUN TO BE A MUSHROOM CLOUD.
RICE'S COLLEAGUES WERE SURPRISED TO SEE THE "CAREFUL DIPLOMACY" SHE EXHIBITED IN PRESIDENT GEORGE HW BUSH'S CABINET TURN INTO HAWK-LIKE ATTITUDES ABOUT WAR IN GEORGE W.'S SERVICE.
SOME SUGGEST SHE WAS ILL-PREPARED FOR THE MONUMENTAL TASK OF A NEW KIND OF WAR, WITH A NEW KIND OF ENEMY. THE TERRORISTS MADE HARD-LINE SOVIETS LOOK TAME.
1988
BRENT SCOWCRAFT, WHO LAUNCHED CONDI'S POLITICAL CAREER BY OFFERING HER A JOB IN GEORGE HW BUSH'S CABINET IN 1988, NOW CLASHED WITH HER OVER IRAQ, CALLING HER OUT IN A MUCH-PUBLICIZED EDITORIAL TITLED "DON'T ATTACK SADDAM."
"I DON'T UNDERSTAND HOW MY LADY, MY BABY, MY DISCIPLE, HAS CHANGED SO MUCH," HE LATER SAID.
IT'S ALL VERY SHAKESPEARIAN SOUNDING. OR GEORGE LUCAS-ISH, I SUPPOSE. EVEN CONDI'S STEPMOTHER CLARA IN BIRMINGHAM CONFESSED TO CONDI THAT SHE THOUGHT BIN LADEN WAS WHO THEY WERE AFTER... NOT SADDAM.

I'LL GIVE HER THIS: HAD CONDI BEEN SECRETARY OF STATE IN OBAMA'S CABINET, INSTEAD OF HILLARY CLINTON, RUSSIAN RELATIONS WOULD BE LESS EMBARRASSING.
THE BUTTON IS SYMBOLIC, '*PEREGRUZKA*' MEANS '*RESET*'! SEE?
[ACTUALLY, IT MEANS 'OVERCHARGE.' THANKS FOR PLAYING, CHAMP.]
*TRANSLATED FROM RUSSIAN
BUT HER RUSSIAN EXPERTISE WAS TRUMPED BY **IRAQ**.
HAVE YOU EVER TRIED TO SHOVEL A SIDEWALK WHILE IT'S STILL SNOWING? THIS MIGHT SUM UP CONDI'S WELL-MEANING, BUT ULTIMATELY FAILED, EFFORTS TO STABILIZE IRAQ AND HEAL WOUNDS WITH **US** ENEMIES AND ALLIES.
THE CONSTANT HEAD-BUTTING WITH RUMSFELD, CHENEY AND UNCOOPERATIVE GOVERNMENTAL AGENCIES PROBABLY DIDN'T HELP, EITHER.
RICE NEEDED A GOOD PUBLICITY MANAGER. EVEN SOMETHING AS INNOCENT AS THE CHANCE TO PLAY ALONGSIDE HER HERO YO-YO MA APPEARED TO MANY AS NERO FIDDLING WHILE ROME BURNED.
IT'S WITH SOME IRONY THAT, AS CONDI WAS SHOPPING IN NEW YORK-- SOMETHING HER MOTHER FOUGHT DRAMATICALLY FOR THE RIGHT TO DO--
ARE THOSE FERRAGAMO? I'LL *TAKE* THEM.
THAT NO ONE SAW THE TRIUMPH OF AN AFRICAN AMERICAN WOMAN: THEY SAW AN OUT-OF-TOUCH POLITICIAN SPENDING THOUSANDS ON SHOES, ONE DAY AFTER HURRICANE KATRINA.
NO BLOOD FOR OIL!!!
WHEN THE LEVEE BREAKS I'LL HAVE NO PLACE TO STAY
SECURITY! GET THOSE PEOPLE AWAY FROM THIS STORE! I'M SORRY, MS. RICE... LET ME WRAP THESE FOR YOU.

IN 2007, RICE RETURNED HOME, TO GIVE A SPEECH AT THE UNIVERSITY OF ALABAMA. AN IMPASSIONED PLEA, AND A GLIMPSE INTO WHY A DEMOCRATIC IRAQ WAS SO IMPORTANT TO HER.
IT'S THE VERY HEIGHT OF ARROGANCE TO BELIEVE THAT POLITICAL LIBERTY, AND RIGHTS FOR WOMEN, AND FREEDOM OF SPEECH, AND THE RULE OF THE LAW BELONG ONLY TO US.
"...IT IS TYRANNY, NOT DEMOCRACY, THAT HAS TO BE FORCED UPON PEOPLE AT GUNPOINT."
AND THEN, IT WAS OVER.
DO YOU MISS THE JOB?
NO, I REALLY DON'T!
I AM SO HAPPY TO GET UP IN THE MORNING, READ THE NEWSPAPER, AND NOT THINK I HAVE TO DO ANYTHING ABOUT WHAT'S IN IT.
BUT IT WAS AN HONOR TO SERVE, I LOVE THIS COUNTRY.
AND AS WE WIND ON DOWN THE ROAD! OUR SHADOWS TALLER THAN OUR SO-UUULLL!
AND YET, KNOWING ALL I NOW KNOW ABOUT HER-- ABOUT HER CLASSICALLY-TRAINED MIND AND STRICT UPBRINGING--
I'M LEFT UNFULFILLED.
"IT'S NOT A POPULARITY CONTEST," CONDI SAID OF THE ADMINISTRATION'S LOW APPROVAL RATINGS. FORGOTTEN IN THE SHUFFLE WERE RICE'S SMALLER DIPLOMATIC VICTORIES WITH NORTH KOREA AND LIBYA. THE 1,006,846 MILES LOGGED ON AMERICA'S BEHALF. THE RACIAL AND GENDER BARRIERS SHATTERED BY A GIRL FROM BIRMINGHAM.
SOMEONE TELL ME: WHAT EXACTLY DOES CONDOLEEZZA RICE GET OUT OF LED ZEPPELIN?
ARE YOU KIDDING? IT'S NOT NUCLEAR SCIENCE-- IT'S Zeppelin
EVERYONE LOVES ZEPPELIN.
OH.
PERHAPS I'M OVERTHINKING EVERYTHING.
THE END

COLIN
POWELL

HI THERE. THE NAME'S WEY AND I'LL BE YOUR CAPTIONS, TEXT AND SPEECH BUBBLES FOR THIS ISSUE.
YOU KNOW IT TOOK ME MANY, AND I MEAN MANY, REWRITES TO COME UP WITH THIS INTRODUCTION.
I HAD SOME PRETTY CRAZY IDEAS WHICH I WON'T GO INTO ANY DETAILS ABOUT.
MAYBE I'LL TELL YOU LATER ON WHEN DARREN'S NOT LISTENING IN.
BUT YOU KNOW WHAT I REALIZED.
I DON'T NEED TO GLITZ UP THE STORY OF COLIN POWELL WITH A SUPER-STAGE-SHOW INTRO.
I DON'T NEED ALL THAT JAZZ AND PIZZAZZ.
BECAUSE THIS MAN'S STORY ALREADY HAS IT ALL.
IT'S RICH IN TEXTURE AND ITS DEEP IN EMOTIONS. IT EXPLORES ISSUES THAT HAVE SHAKEN THE FOUNDATIONS OF AMERICAN CULTURE AND SOCIETY.
BUT THIS IS NOT JUST A STORY OF ONE MAN, IT'S ALSO A STORY OF A NATION. OF HOW AMERICA GREW UP AND MATURED INTO THE DEMOCRATIC SOCIETY OF TODAY.
SO WITHOUT FURTHER ADO.
LET US BEGIN.
BLUEWATER PRODUCTIONS

HE IS PERHAPS ONE OF THE MOST PROMINENT AFRICAN AMERICAN FIGURES TO SERVE UNDER THE UNITED STATES FLAG.
WELCOME
ALTHOUGH HE HAD ALWAYS BEEN A RESPECTED PUBLIC LEADER ON MILITARY MATTERS, HE SHOT INTO THE MEDIA SPOTLIGHT AND GAINED A ROCK-STAR-LIKE STATUS FOLLOWING HIS SUCCESS AS CHAIRMAN OF THE JOINT CHIEFS OF STAFF DURING THE PERSIAN GULF WAR OF THE EARLY 90S.
OTHERWISE KNOWN AS OPERATION DESERT STORM.
AT THE HEIGHT OF HIS CAREER, COLIN POWELL WAS THE MOST TRUSTED AND RESPECTED MAN IN AMERICA.
SO TRUSTED IN FACT, THAT THE NATION WANTED HIM TO RUN FOR PRESIDENT.

ON MONDAY, NOVEMBER 16TH, 2004, THE TABLES HAD TURNED. COLIN POWELL WAS NOW AT THE LOWEST POINT IN HIS CAREER.
FOLLOWING THE REELECTION OF GEORGE W BUSH INTO HIS SECOND TERM OF OFFICE, COLIN POWELL, THE FOUR STAR GENERAL AND SECRETARY OF STATE, HAS ANNOUNCED HIS RESIGNATION.
THIS ENDS A TUMULTUOUS TERM FOR GENERAL POWELL, HAVING SERVING 4 YEARS UNDER GEORGE W. BUSH.
HIS SUPPORT OF BUSH IN THE LEAD UP TO THE IRAQ INVASION WAS CRITICIZED BY MANY AFTER IT WAS DISCOVERED THAT THE DOCUMENT HE PRESENTED TO THE UN CONFIRMING SADDAM HUSSEIN'S NUCLEAR CAPABILITIES, WAS FALSE.
THE MISTAKE THAT WAS THE IRAQ WAR IS ONE THAT WILL NOT BE EASILY FORGOTTEN BY GENERAL POWELL, LET ALONE THIS NATION.
SOUTH BRONX
FURNITURE
POWELL WAS LEAVING THE WHITE HOUSE AND HIS CAREER IN POLITICS - AND NOT ON GOOD TERMS.
GOOD RIDDANCE I SAY. IT WAS HIS FAULT WE WENT TO WAR IN IRAQ. WHAT GOOD DID THAT DO. HIS FAULT WE ARE BEING--
SHUT YOUR MOUTH YOUNG MAN. YOU DON'T EVEN KNOW THE MAN. YOU DON'T KNOW HIS WHOLE STORY. HE'S DONE PLENTY FOR THIS NATION. PUT HIS LIFE AT RISK FOR THE BETTERMENT OF OUR NATION. SHOW SOME RESPECT.

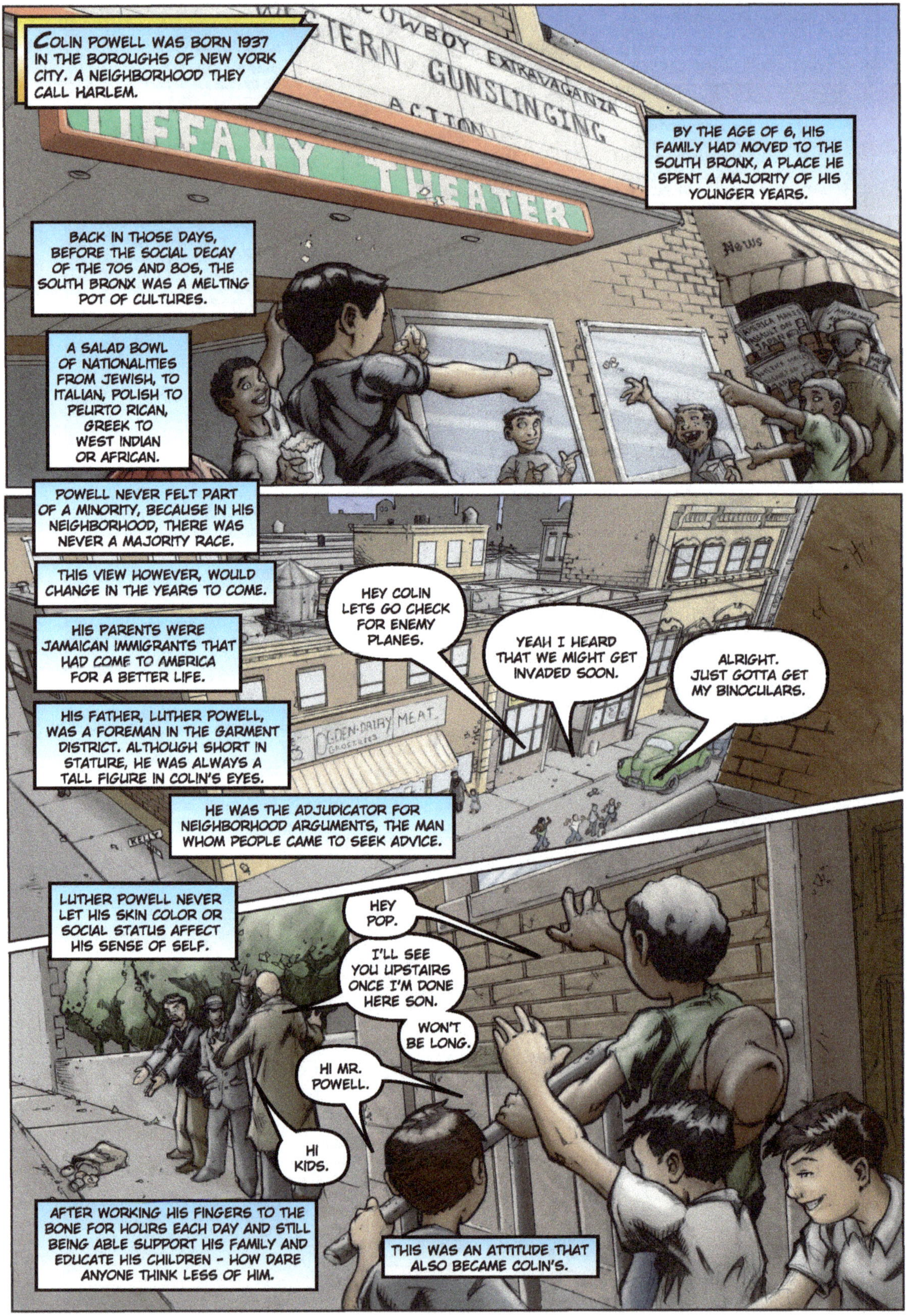
COLIN POWELL WAS BORN 1937 IN THE BOROUGHS OF NEW YORK CITY. A NEIGHBORHOOD THEY CALL HARLEM.
WESTERN COWBOY EXTRAVAGANZA
GUNSLINGING ACTION
TIFFANY THEATER
BY THE AGE OF 6, HIS FAMILY HAD MOVED TO THE SOUTH BRONX, A PLACE HE SPENT A MAJORITY OF HIS YOUNGER YEARS.
BACK IN THOSE DAYS, BEFORE THE SOCIAL DECAY OF THE 70S AND 80S, THE SOUTH BRONX WAS A MELTING POT OF CULTURES.
A SALAD BOWL OF NATIONALITIES FROM JEWISH, TO ITALIAN, POLISH TO PEURTO RICAN, GREEK TO WEST INDIAN OR AFRICAN.
News
POWELL NEVER FELT PART OF A MINORITY, BECAUSE IN HIS NEIGHBORHOOD, THERE WAS NEVER A MAJORITY RACE.
THIS VIEW HOWEVER, WOULD CHANGE IN THE YEARS TO COME.
HIS PARENTS WERE JAMAICAN IMMIGRANTS THAT HAD COME TO AMERICA FOR A BETTER LIFE.
HIS FATHER, LUTHER POWELL, WAS A FOREMAN IN THE GARMENT DISTRICT. ALTHOUGH SHORT IN STATURE, HE WAS ALWAYS A TALL FIGURE IN COLIN'S EYES.
HEY COLIN LETS GO CHECK FOR ENEMY PLANES.
YEAH I HEARD THAT WE MIGHT GET INVADED SOON.
ALRIGHT. JUST GOTTA GET MY BINOCULARS.
OGDEN DAIRY
MEAT
GROCERIES
HE WAS THE ADJUDICATOR FOR NEIGHBORHOOD ARGUMENTS, THE MAN WHOM PEOPLE CAME TO SEEK ADVICE.
LUTHER POWELL NEVER LET HIS SKIN COLOR OR SOCIAL STATUS AFFECT HIS SENSE OF SELF.
HEY POP.
I'LL SEE YOU UPSTAIRS ONCE I'M DONE HERE SON.
WON'T BE LONG.
HI MR. POWELL.
HI KIDS.
AFTER WORKING HIS FINGERS TO THE BONE FOR HOURS EACH DAY AND STILL BEING ABLE SUPPORT HIS FAMILY AND EDUCATE HIS CHILDREN - HOW DARE ANYONE THINK LESS OF HIM.
THIS WAS AN ATTITUDE THAT ALSO BECAME COLIN'S.

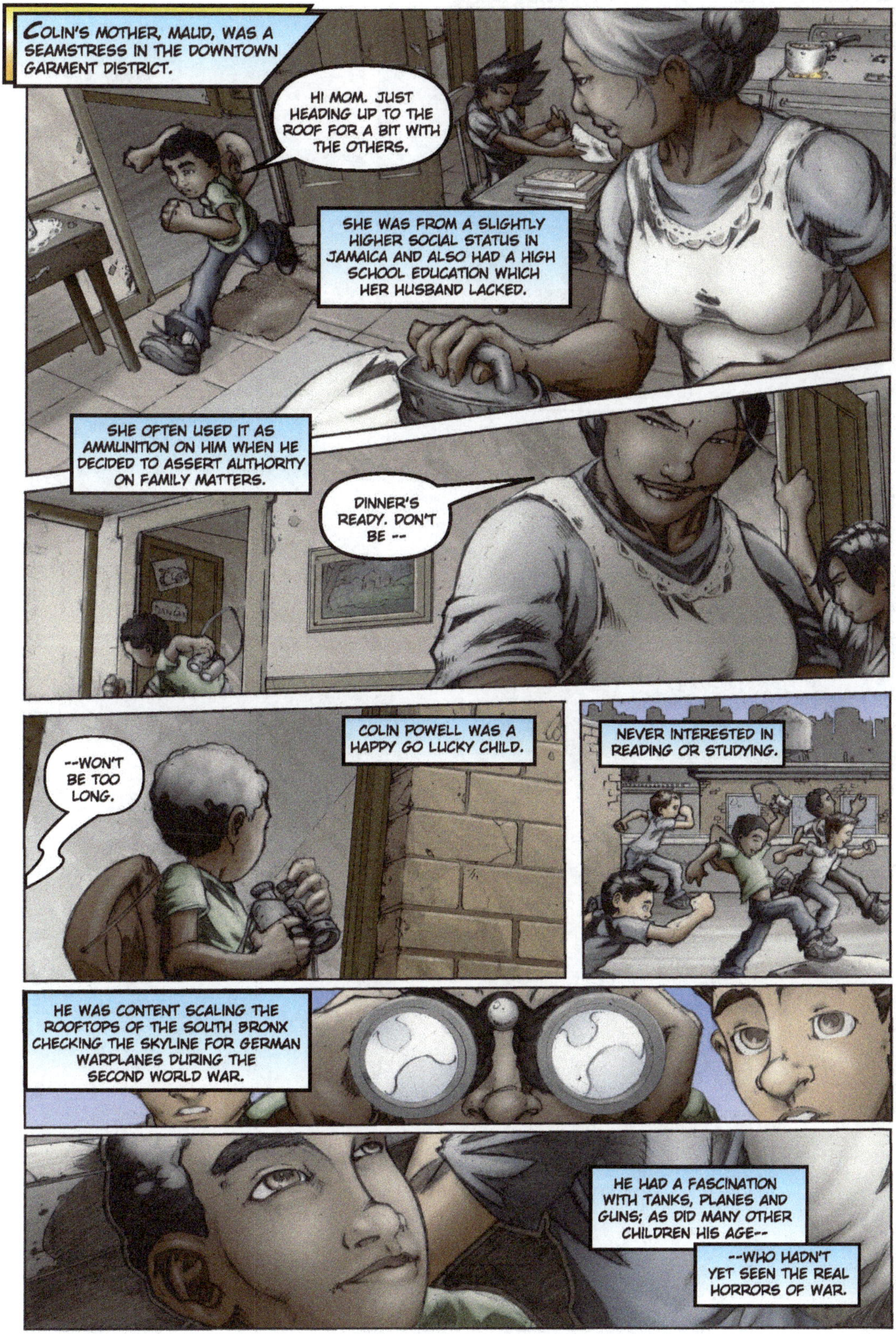
COLIN'S MOTHER, MAUD, WAS A SEAMSTRESS IN THE DOWNTOWN GARMENT DISTRICT.
HI MOM. JUST HEADING UP TO THE ROOF FOR A BIT WITH THE OTHERS.
SHE WAS FROM A SLIGHTLY HIGHER SOCIAL STATUS IN JAMAICA AND ALSO HAD A HIGH SCHOOL EDUCATION WHICH HER HUSBAND LACKED.
SHE OFTEN USED IT AS AMMUNITION ON HIM WHEN HE DECIDED TO ASSERT AUTHORITY ON FAMILY MATTERS.
DINNER'S READY. DON'T BE --
--WON'T BE TOO LONG.
COLIN POWELL WAS A HAPPY GO LUCKY CHILD.
NEVER INTERESTED IN READING OR STUDYING.
HE WAS CONTENT SCALING THE ROOFTOPS OF THE SOUTH BRONX CHECKING THE SKYLINE FOR GERMAN WARPLANES DURING THE SECOND WORLD WAR.
HE HAD A FASCINATION WITH TANKS, PLANES AND GUNS; AS DID MANY OTHER CHILDREN HIS AGE--
--WHO HADN'T YET SEEN THE REAL HORRORS OF WAR.

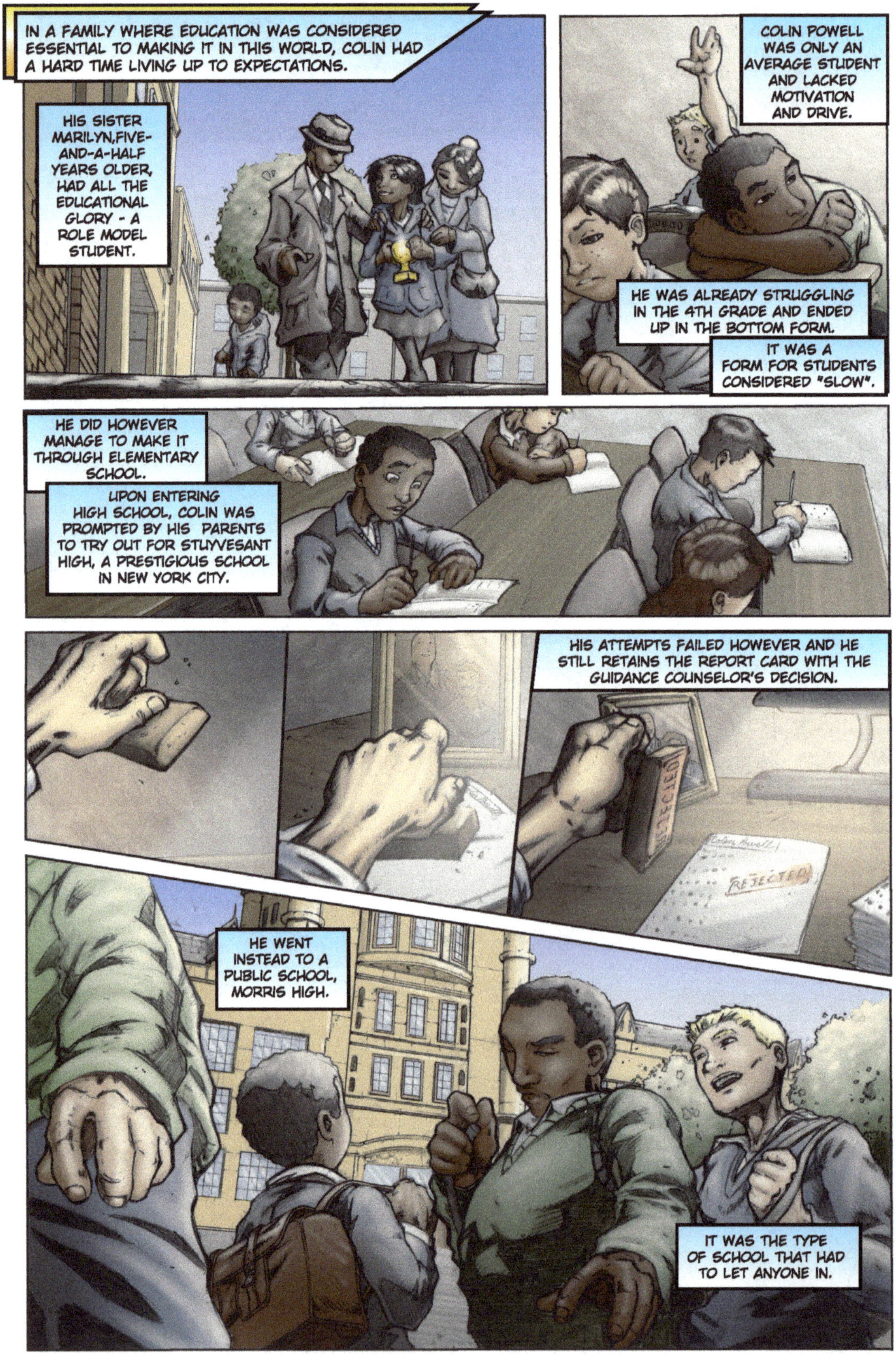
IN A FAMILY WHERE EDUCATION WAS CONSIDERED ESSENTIAL TO MAKING IT IN THIS WORLD, COLIN HAD A HARD TIME LIVING UP TO EXPECTATIONS.
HIS SISTER MARILYN, FIVE-AND-A-HALF YEARS OLDER, HAD ALL THE EDUCATIONAL GLORY - A ROLE MODEL STUDENT.
COLIN POWELL WAS ONLY AN AVERAGE STUDENT AND LACKED MOTIVATION AND DRIVE.
HE WAS ALREADY STRUGGLING IN THE 4TH GRADE AND ENDED UP IN THE BOTTOM FORM.
IT WAS A FORM FOR STUDENTS CONSIDERED "SLOW".
HE DID HOWEVER MANAGE TO MAKE IT THROUGH ELEMENTARY SCHOOL.
UPON ENTERING HIGH SCHOOL, COLIN WAS PROMPTED BY HIS PARENTS TO TRY OUT FOR STUYVESANT HIGH, A PRESTIGIOUS SCHOOL IN NEW YORK CITY.
HIS ATTEMPTS FAILED HOWEVER AND HE STILL RETAINS THE REPORT CARD WITH THE GUIDANCE COUNSELOR'S DECISION.
Colin Powell
REJECTED
HE WENT INSTEAD TO A PUBLIC SCHOOL, MORRIS HIGH.
IT WAS THE TYPE OF SCHOOL THAT HAD TO LET ANYONE IN.

HE EVENTUALLY GRADUATED AT THE AGE OF 17, THANKS TO AN ACCELERATED PROGRAM, "RATHER THEN ANY BRILLIANCE" ON HIS PART.
BUT COLIN WAS STILL DIRECTIONLESS AND HIS PARENTS WERE BECOMING INCREASINGLY CONCERNED.
A COLLEGE EDUCATION IS YOUR WAY TO A BETTER LIFE. LOOK HOW WELL YOUR SISTER HAS DONE.
GO ON SON. YOU CAN DO IT.
ONCE AGAIN, UNDER THE INFLUENCE OF HIS PARENTS, POWELL DECIDED TO ENTER COLLEGE AT CITY COLLEGE NEW YORK, OR CCNY.
THIS IS WHERE HIS DESTINY WOULD CHANGE.
IN HIS FIRST SEMESTER AT CCNY, COLIN WAS DRAWN TO THE ROTC, OR THE RESERVE OFFICERS' TRAINING CORPS.
HE DECIDED TO JOIN.
WHEN ISSUED HIS OWN UNIFORM AND TRYING IT ON FOR THE FIRST TIME, HE FELT DISTINCTIVE.
MANY OF HIS FRIENDS HAD OPTED NOT TO GO INTO COLLEGE AND THIS HAD LEFT COLIN FEELING LONELY AND ISOLATED.
THE UNIFORM GAVE HIM A SENSE OF BELONGING.
IT WAS IN THE RANKS OF THIS SYSTEM THAT HE FELT LIKE HE COULD TAKE DIRECTION.
THE ROTC WAS LIKE A BROTHERHOOD TO HIM AND HE ENJOYED THE STRUCTURE, DISCIPLINE AND CAMARADERIE IT OFFERED.
LIKE HE COULD LEAD.

IN THE SUMMER OF 1957 POWELL WENT OFF TO ROTC SUMMER CAMP AT FORT BRAGG, NORTH CAROLINA.
HIS FIRST JOURNEY INTO THE SOUTH.
IT WAS A SUMMER THAT ENDED IN A BITTERSWEET VICTORY.
COLIN WAS NAMED "BEST CADET COMPANY D" AND ALSO CAME SECOND IN THE CATEGORY OF BEST CADET FOR THE ENTIRE ENCAMPMENT.
HE WAS FEELING WONDERFUL AND HAD A SENSE THAT HE HAD FINALLY EXCELLED.
HIS MOMENT OF GLORY WAS SOON TO BE CRUSHED.
YOU KNOW WHY YOU'RE ONLY THE SECOND BEST CADET IN CAMP?
DO YOU THINK THESE SOUTHERN ROTC INSTRUCTORS ARE GOING TO GO BACK TO THEIR COLLEGES AND TELL THEM THAT THE BEST KID HERE WAS BLACK?
COLIN WAS STUNNED MORE THEN ANGERED.
THIS WAS HIS FIRST EXPERIENCE OF THE CRUEL TASTE OF RACISM.
ON THE WAY HOME HE DIDN'T FEEL SAFE.
IT WASN'T TILL HE REACHED WASHINGTON THAT HE COULD BEGIN TO RELAX.
AFTER THIS DEGRADING EPISODE, COLIN COULD HAVE GIVEN UP ON THE ARMY. BUT HE DIDN'T.
IN JUNE OF 1958, HE BECAME A DISTINGUISHED MILITARY GRADUATE.
HIS PARENTS COULD FINALLY BE PROUD OF HIM.
HE WAS NO LONGER THE AIMLESS AND DIRECTIONLESS KID FROM THE SOUTH BRONX.
HE WAS LIEUTENANT POWELL, OFFICER OF THE UNITED STATES ARMY.

WHAT IS LIFE BUT A SERIES OF UPS AND DOWN, A ROAD OF TWISTS AND TURNS.
Fort Benning Army Reserve
COLIN WAS SOON STATIONED BACK IN THE DEEP SOUTH AT FORT BENNING, GEORGIA.
ON THE BRIGHT SIDE, THE ARMY HAD BEEN DESEGREGATED SINCE 1948 THANKS TO PRESIDENT TRUMAN.
AT THE ARMY POST, EVERYONE WAS TREATED EQUALLY.
LIFE OUTSIDE THE POST WAS A DIFFERENT STORY.
IN THE SOUTH, MANY BASIC HUMAN RIGHTS AND PRIVILEGES WERE TAKEN AWAY IF YOU HAPPENED TO BE BLACK.
WOOLWORTH'S
PHARMACY
DON'T EVEN THINK ABOUT IT SON.
THOSE TABLES ARE FOR WHITE FOLK ONLY.
NOW YOU TAKE YOUR SHOPPING AND RUN ALONG NOW.
HE WAS ONLY ABLE TO SHOP AT THE GROCERY STORE IF HE DIDNT SIT DOWN TO EAT.
HE WOULD ONLY BE ALLOWED INTO A DEPARTMENT STORE AS LONG AS HE DIDN'T TRY TO USE THE MENS ROOM.
Colored
AND HE COULD WALK DOWN THE STREET AS LONG AS HE DIDNT LOOK AT A WHITE WOMAN.
IT WAS ALWAYS A HURTFUL EXPERIENCE FOR POWELL BUT HE DID HIS BEST NOT TO LET IT GET TO HIM.
HE DIDN'T WANT TO BECOME A VICTIM OF BIGOTRY.

IN NOVEMBER OF 1961 COLIN POWELL WENT ALONG WITH A FRIEND ON A BLIND DATE AND MET THE SOFT SPEAKING SOUTHERNER, ALMA JOHNSON.
NEW YEAR
HE WAS ENCHANTED BY HER EYES THE FIRST TIME HE GLANCED AT THEM.
THEY FREQUENTLY DATED AND SOON AFTER A MONTH, COLIN WAS INTRODUCING HER TO HIS "NOISY" AND "FUN LOVING" FAMILY.
THE TWO WERE INSEPARABLE.
BUT BY AUGUST OF 1962 HE WAS ORDERED TO VIETNAM TO SERVE AS A MILITARY ADVISER.
ALMA WAS UPSET AND UNSURE WHAT THAT MEANT FOR THEIR FUTURE TOGETHER.
WE CAN STILL WRITE TO EACH OTHER.
I'M NOT GOING TO BE YOUR PENPAL
WE MIGHT AS WELL END IT NOW.
COLIN LEFT THAT NIGHT DEJECTED.
BUT HE SOON REALIZED THAT HE COULDN'T LET THE LOVE OF HIS LIFE GETAWAY THAT EASY.
YES!!
ON SATURDAY, AUGUST 25, 1962, TWO WEEKS AFTER HIS PROPOSAL, ALMA JOHNSON WAS NOW ALMA POWELL.
COLIN AND ALMA'S MARRIAGE IS CONSIDERED TO BE ONE OF THE STRONGEST IN AMERICAN POLITICS.
THEY WENT ON TO HAVE THREE CHILDREN. MICHAEL, LINDA AND ANNE.

WHAT'S YOUR'S IS ALSO MINE.
BACK IN THE 1960S, COMMUNISM WAS CONSIDERED AN EVIL BY WESTERN COUNTRIES, THE USA IN PARTICULAR.
OH THANK GOD THE AMERICANS HAVE ARRIVED!!
FREEDOM REIGNS ONCE MORE!!
THE COLD WAR BATTLE BETWEEN COMMUNIST RUSSIA AND CAPITALIST AMERICA HAD BEEN GOING ON FOR YEARS SINCE THE END OF WORLD WAR 2.
IT SEEMED NOW THAT THE IDEOLOGIES OF MARXISM WERE SEEPING INTO THE SOUTH EAST ASIAN REGION OF VIETNAM.
THE US WERE AFRAID THAT THE FALL OF VIETNAM TO THE HANDS OF COMMUNISTS WOULD LEAD TO THE COLLAPSE OF SURROUNDING TERRITORIES.
THE COMMUNIST NORTH WAS AIMING TO OVER THROW THE FRENCH BACKED GOVERNMENT OF SOUTH VIETNAM. AMERICA HAD TO INTERVENE.
BY 1963, PRESIDENT KENNEDY HAD SENT 16000 MILITARY ADVISORS TO SOUTH VIETNAM TO PROVIDE TRAINING AND ASSISTANCE TO THE ARVN (ARMY OF THE REPUBLIC OF VIETNAM).
ON JAN 17, 1963, COLIN POWELL LANDED AT HIS BASE IN A SHAU VALLEY. HE WAS EXCITED AT THE PROSPECT OF FIGHTING FOR A NOBLE CAUSE.
BUT THAT WAS ALL IT WAS. A PROSPECT.
AND SOON HE WOULD FIND OUT WHAT WAR REALLY WAS.
UP CLOSE AND PERSONAL.

COLIN'S FIRST TASTE OF THE HARSH REALITIES OF WARFARE CAME DURING A PROLONGED PATROL OF THE A SHAU VALLEY.
DIDN'T YOU HEAR WHAT I -
TRY TO SPREAD OUT.
DON'T STAY SINGLE FILE GODDAMN IT.
HIS BATTALION WAS AMBUSHED ALMOST DAILY BY THE VIET CONG -
- A FACELESS ENEMY THEY WERE STILL YET TO SEE.
WHILE COLIN WAS DODGING BULLETS IN A SHAU, ALMA AND HER PARENTS WERE DODGING THE ATTACKS OF WHITE SUPREMACISTS IN BIRMINGHAM, ALABAMA.
RACIAL TENSIONS HAD IGNITED IN THE SOUTH AND BIRMINGHAM WAS DEEMED THE WORST CITY IN AMERICA.
BOMBINGS OF BLACK HOMES AND CHURCHES WERE BECOMING A USUAL OCCURRENCE.
ALMA WAS EXPECTING THEIR CHILD ANY DAY NOW AND HER FATHER, RC, HAD TO STAY UP AT NIGHT WITH A SHOTGUN ACROSS HIS LAP IN FEAR OF WHO WOULD COME THROUGH THEIR FRONT DOOR.
WE COME TO YOU LIVE FROM THE STREETS OF BIRMINGHAM. A TOWN THAT HAS JUST ERUPTED INTO CHAOS.
THOUSANDS OF BLACK MEN, WOMEN AND CHILDREN HAVE DESCENDED ON TO THE STREETS AT THE TOWN'S CENTER IN PROTEST OF THEIR UNFAIR TREATMENT IN WHITE AMERICA.
THE POLICE HAVE RESPONDED WITH A FORCE MANY DEEM INAPPROPRIATE AND VIOLENT.
EVEN CHILDREN IN THE TOWNS CENTER ARE BEING BEING ARRESTED.
THIS WAS HARDLY THE TIME OR PLACE TO BRING A CHILD INTO THE WORLD.
BUT NEVERTHELESS, ON MARCH 23, 1963, MICHAEL KEVIN POWELL CAME INTO THE WORLD AT THE HOLY FAMILY CATHOLIC HOSPITAL, BIRMINGHAM.
WHAT IS THIS WORLD COMING TO?
ON MAY 7, 1963, BIRMINGHAM REACHED CRISIS POINT AND THE CITY COLLAPSED INTO CHAOS.

BACK IN THE JUNGLES OF VIETNAM, THE TOLL OF THE DEAD AND WOUNDED WAS MOUNTING.
THERE WERE STILL NO SIGHTINGS OF THE ENEMY. JUST THE SPRAY OF BULLETS THEY LEFT IN THEIR WAKE.
WAR WAS NOTHING LIKE THE SATURDAY AFTERNOON MOVIES COLIN USE TO WATCH AT THE TIFFANY THEATRE.
COLIN WITNESSED COUNTLESS DEATHS.
EACH OF WHICH AFFECTED HIM GREATLY.
STRANGELY ENOUGH, FOLLOWING EACH DEATH, COLIN WOULD AWAKE REFRESHED AND INVIGORATED THE NEXT MORNING.
THIS PHENOMENON WAS COMMON AMONG MEN EXPERIENCING THE BRUTALITIES OF WAR.
IT HELPED SHAPE HIS ATTITUDE THAT IN WAKE OF THE MOST DARKEST AND TERRIFYING NIGHT, YOU CAN BE REASSURED THAT THINGS WILL ALWAYS LOOK BETTER IN THE MORNING.

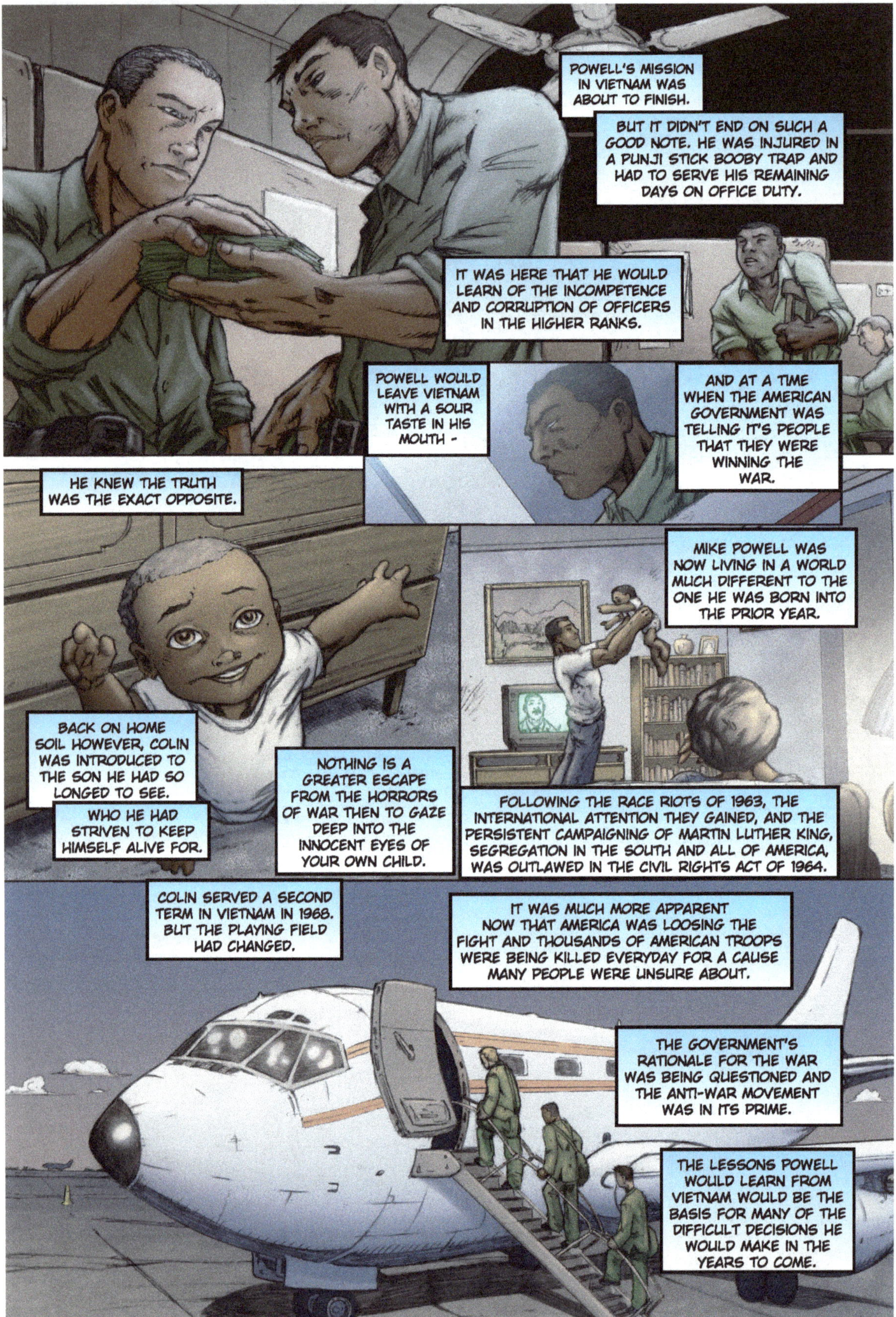
POWELL'S MISSION IN VIETNAM WAS ABOUT TO FINISH.
BUT IT DIDN'T END ON SUCH A GOOD NOTE. HE WAS INJURED IN A PUNJI STICK BOOBY TRAP AND HAD TO SERVE HIS REMAINING DAYS ON OFFICE DUTY.
IT WAS HERE THAT HE WOULD LEARN OF THE INCOMPETENCE AND CORRUPTION OF OFFICERS IN THE HIGHER RANKS.
POWELL WOULD LEAVE VIETNAM WITH A SOUR TASTE IN HIS MOUTH -
AND AT A TIME WHEN THE AMERICAN GOVERNMENT WAS TELLING IT'S PEOPLE THAT THEY WERE WINNING THE WAR.
HE KNEW THE TRUTH WAS THE EXACT OPPOSITE.
MIKE POWELL WAS NOW LIVING IN A WORLD MUCH DIFFERENT TO THE ONE HE WAS BORN INTO THE PRIOR YEAR.
BACK ON HOME SOIL HOWEVER, COLIN WAS INTRODUCED TO THE SON HE HAD SO LONGED TO SEE.
WHO HE HAD STRIVEN TO KEEP HIMSELF ALIVE FOR.
NOTHING IS A GREATER ESCAPE FROM THE HORRORS OF WAR THEN TO GAZE DEEP INTO THE INNOCENT EYES OF YOUR OWN CHILD.
FOLLOWING THE RACE RIOTS OF 1963, THE INTERNATIONAL ATTENTION THEY GAINED, AND THE PERSISTENT CAMPAIGNING OF MARTIN LUTHER KING, SEGREGATION IN THE SOUTH AND ALL OF AMERICA, WAS OUTLAWED IN THE CIVIL RIGHTS ACT OF 1964.
COLIN SERVED A SECOND TERM IN VIETNAM IN 1968. BUT THE PLAYING FIELD HAD CHANGED.
IT WAS MUCH MORE APPARENT NOW THAT AMERICA WAS LOOSING THE FIGHT AND THOUSANDS OF AMERICAN TROOPS WERE BEING KILLED EVERYDAY FOR A CAUSE MANY PEOPLE WERE UNSURE ABOUT.
THE GOVERNMENT'S RATIONALE FOR THE WAR WAS BEING QUESTIONED AND THE ANTI-WAR MOVEMENT WAS IN ITS PRIME.
THE LESSONS POWELL WOULD LEARN FROM VIETNAM WOULD BE THE BASIS FOR MANY OF THE DIFFICULT DECISIONS HE WOULD MAKE IN THE YEARS TO COME.

FOLLOWING THE VIETNAM YEARS, COLIN POWELL WOULD RISE THROUGH THE RANKS OF THE UNITED STATES MILITARY.
IN JUNE OF 1979 HE RECEIVED HIS FIRST STAR MAKING HIM A BRIGADIER GENERAL.
HE WAS NOW ALSO THE YOUNGEST GENERAL IN THE ARMY AT AGE 42.
IT WAS A SHAME THAT HIS FATHER WAS UNABLE TO ATTEND HIS PROMOTION CEREMONY. LUTHER POWELL, THE PRINCIPLE FIGURE IN COLIN'S LIFE, HAD PASSED AWAY THE YEAR BEFORE AFTER A BATTLE WITH CANCER. HE WOULD HAVE BEEN PROUD OF HIS SON.
5 YEARS LATER, IN 1984, MAUD ARIEL POWELL WOULD LOSE THE SAME FIGHT TO CANCER. SHE WAS ABOUT TO MISS OUT ON THE EXCITEMENT OF THE YEARS TO COME.
COLIN RECEIVED HIS SECOND STAR IN 1983.
HIS THIRD IN 1986.
BUT IN NOVEMBER 23, 1987, HE WOULD ASSUME HIS BIGGEST ROLE YET.
PERHAPS THE HIGHEST ROLE ANY AFRICAN AMERICAN HAD YET ACHIEVED.
COLIN POWELL WAS THE NATIONAL SECURITY ADVISOR TO RONALD REAGAN.
AS THE FIRST AFRICAN AMERICAN IN THIS POSITION HE FELT PROUD, BUT AT THE SAME TIME HE FELT A PRESSURE TO PROVE HIMSELF. EVEN SO, IT WAS STILL PROOF THAT HIS COUNTRY HAD COME A LONG WAY SINCE THE DAYS HE SERVED AS A SECOND LIEUTENANT IN THE OLD SOUTH AT FORT BENNING.

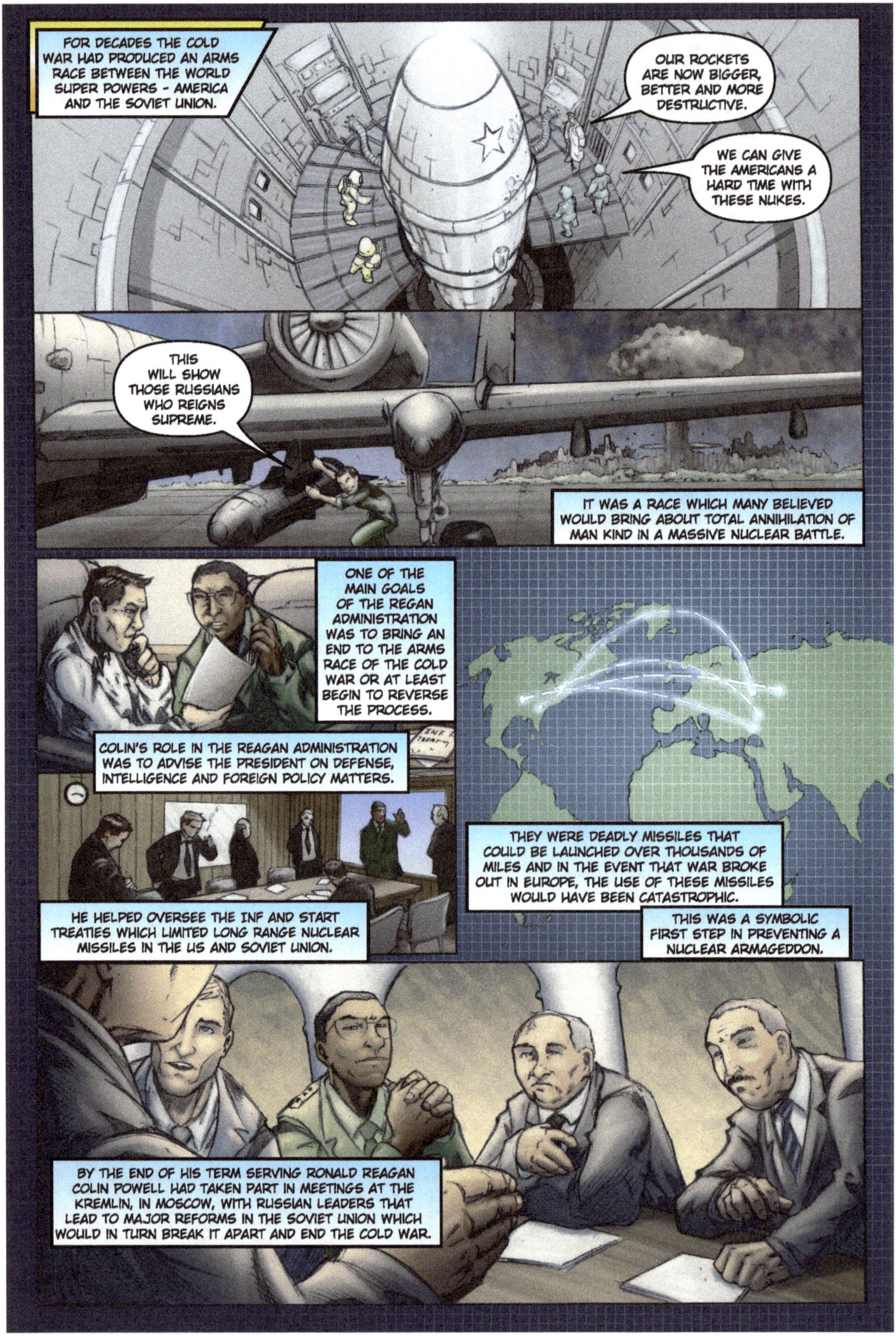
FOR DECADES THE COLD WAR HAD PRODUCED AN ARMS RACE BETWEEN THE WORLD SUPER POWERS - AMERICA AND THE SOVIET UNION.
OUR ROCKETS ARE NOW BIGGER, BETTER AND MORE DESTRUCTIVE.
WE CAN GIVE THE AMERICANS A HARD TIME WITH THESE NUKES.
THIS WILL SHOW THOSE RUSSIANS WHO REIGNS SUPREME.
IT WAS A RACE WHICH MANY BELIEVED WOULD BRING ABOUT TOTAL ANNIHILATION OF MAN KIND IN A MASSIVE NUCLEAR BATTLE.
ONE OF THE MAIN GOALS OF THE REGAN ADMINISTRATION WAS TO BRING AN END TO THE ARMS RACE OF THE COLD WAR OR AT LEAST BEGIN TO REVERSE THE PROCESS.
COLIN'S ROLE IN THE REAGAN ADMINISTRATION WAS TO ADVISE THE PRESIDENT ON DEFENSE, INTELLIGENCE AND FOREIGN POLICY MATTERS.
HE HELPED OVERSEE THE INF AND START TREATIES WHICH LIMITED LONG RANGE NUCLEAR MISSILES IN THE US AND SOVIET UNION.
THEY WERE DEADLY MISSILES THAT COULD BE LAUNCHED OVER THOUSANDS OF MILES AND IN THE EVENT THAT WAR BROKE OUT IN EUROPE, THE USE OF THESE MISSILES WOULD HAVE BEEN CATASTROPHIC.
THIS WAS A SYMBOLIC FIRST STEP IN PREVENTING A NUCLEAR ARMAGEDDON.
BY THE END OF HIS TERM SERVING RONALD REAGAN COLIN POWELL HAD TAKEN PART IN MEETINGS AT THE KREMLIN, IN MOSCOW, WITH RUSSIAN LEADERS THAT LEAD TO MAJOR REFORMS IN THE SOVIET UNION WHICH WOULD IN TURN BREAK IT APART AND END THE COLD WAR.

TENSIONS BETWEEN KUWAIT AND IRAQ HAVE ESCALATED.
IRAQ HAS ACCUSED KUWAIT, IT'S ONCE NEIGHBOURING FRIEND, OF BEING A GREEDY LAP DOG OF THE WEST -
- AND HOLDS IT RESPONSIBLE FOR BEING UNABLE TO PAY BACK IT'S $90 BILLION DOLLAR DEFICIT ACCRUED OVER THE IRAN-IRAQ WAR OF THE EIGHTIES.
ON OCTOBER 1, 1989, COLIN POWELL, NOW A FOUR STAR GENERAL, WAS APPOINTED CHAIRMAN OF THE JOINT CHIEFS OF STAFF.
HE WOULD SERVE THIS TITLE UNDER THE PRESIDENT GEORGE H.W BUSH.
DURING HIS TIME AS CHAIRMAN HE OVERSAW 28 CRISES.
THE MOST IMPORTANT AND THE ONE HE IS MOST REMEMBERED FOR, WAS THE PERSIAN GULF WAR OF THE EARLY 90S.
IT WAS A DIFFERENT WAR THEN THE IRAQ WAR OF RECENT YEARS.
BUT THE DICTATOR AT THE EPICENTER OF ALL THE COMMOTION WAS THE SAME.
SADDAM HUSSEIN, IRAQI PRESIDENT, HAS ORDERED THOUSANDS OF TROOPS INTO KUWAIT TERRITORY.
HE ALWAYS SOUGHT DIPLOMACY BEFORE WAR.
IT WAS IN HIS ROLE AS CHAIRMAN OF THE JOINT CHIEFS THAT POWELL WOULD EARN HIS NICKNAME AS THE RELUCTANT WARRIOR.
AS THE BUILD UP CONTINUES, LEADERS AROUND THE WORLD ARE CONDEMNING THE ACT.
AFTER THE MISTAKES HE WITNESSED DURING THE VIETNAM WAR AND THE UNNECESSARY LIVES LOST FOR AN OBJECTIVE THE AMERICAN PEOPLE HAD NO UNDERSTANDING ABOUT, COLIN DID NOT WANT TO REPEAT THE SAME MISTAKES.
HE FELT AMERICAN LIVES WERE TOO PRECIOUS A COMMODITY.
BUT THE DIPLOMATIC OPTIONS IN IRAQ HAD WORN OUT.
THIS FORCE IS ENORMOUS. ALL THE SIGNS ARE THERE.
HE HASN'T BUDGED SINCE THE SANCTIONS.
HE'S GOING TO ATTACK.
ALRIGHT, LET'S ARRANGE A MEETING WITH THE PRESIDENT.
WE'RE GOING TO HAVE TO GATHER A LARGE COALITION FORCE IF WE'RE GOING TO DO THIS.

IN RESPONSE TO SADDAM'S FAILURE TO WITHDRAW HIS ARMY, COLIN HELPED COORDINATE A RELATIVELY QUICK AND SUCCESSFUL OFFENSIVE MISSION THAT WOULD BE DUBBED "OPERATION DESERT STORM".
ON FEBRUARY 26, 1991, WITH THE BACKING OF THE UNITED NATIONS, THE US AND OTHER COALITION NATIONS LAUNCHED A SERIES OF AIR AND GROUND ATTACKS ON THE IRAQ ARMY -
FORCING SADDAM'S TROOPS TO FLEE KUWAIT ALONG THE IRAQ-KUWAIT ROAD - HIGHWAY 80.
HOWEVER, IT WAS HERE THAT THE US AIR FORCE UNLEASHED A CONTROVERSIAL STRIKE ON THE FLEEING TROOPS THAT WOULD LATER SPARK AN INTERNATIONAL OUTCRY.
THE PRESS HAD DUBBED THIS ROAD, "THE HIGHWAY OF DEATH".
ON FEB 27, AFTER SEEING THE IMAGES OF OVER ONE THOUSAND CHARRED VEHICLES ALONG THIS ROAD, COLIN KNEW THAT IT WAS TIME TO END THE WAR.
MR. PRESIDENT.
I THINK IT'S TIME TO END THIS THING.
WE DON'T WANT TO BE SEEN AS KILLING FOR KILLINGS SAKE.
YOU'RE RIGHT.
LET'S END IT TODAY.

IN SEPTEMBER,1993, COLIN POWELL HAD REACHED THE END OF A 35 YEAR SERVICE IN THE ARMY.
HE RETIRED AS CHAIRMAN OF THE JOINT CHIEFS OF STAFF. ALTHOUGH HIS MILITARY CAREER WAS ENDING HIS POLITICAL CAREER WAS JUST IN IT'S BEGINNINGS.
WITH THE SUCCESS OF DESERT STORM, COLIN POWELL WAS THROWN INTO THE SPOTLIGHT AND HAD BECOME AN AMERICAN HERO.
IN 1995, FOLLOWING THE RELEASE OF HIS AUTOBIOGRAPHY, "MY AMERICAN JOURNEY," THERE WAS TALK OF POWELL RUNNING FOR THE 1996 PRESIDENCY.
POLLS WERE INDICATING THAT IF HE ENTERED THE RACE, HE HAD A GOOD CHANCE OF WINNING.
HOWEVER, ALMA FEARED FOR THE SAFETY OF HER HUSBAND IF HE WAS TO RUN FOR THE PRESIDENCY.
ON NOVEMBER 9, 1995, HE OFFICIALLY CONFIRMED HE DID NOT INTEND TO RUN IN THE 1996 ELECTION.
HIS REASONS WERE A LACK OF PASSION FOR POLITICS AND THAT HE FELT IT WAS IN THE BEST INTERESTS OF HIS FAMILY.
FOR THE NEXT FEW YEARS, COLIN POWELL MOVED AWAY FROM THE POLITICAL ARENA AND CONCENTRATED ON WORKING WITH THE YOUTH FOUNDATION HE AND ALMA FORMED IN 1997 -
- AMERICA'S PROMISE.
THE FOUNDATION PROVIDED FIVE PROMISES TO CHILDREN AND YOUTH.
CARING ADULTS. SAFE PLACES, A HEALTHY START, AN EFFECTIVE EDUCATION, AND OPPORTUNITIES TO HELP OTHERS.

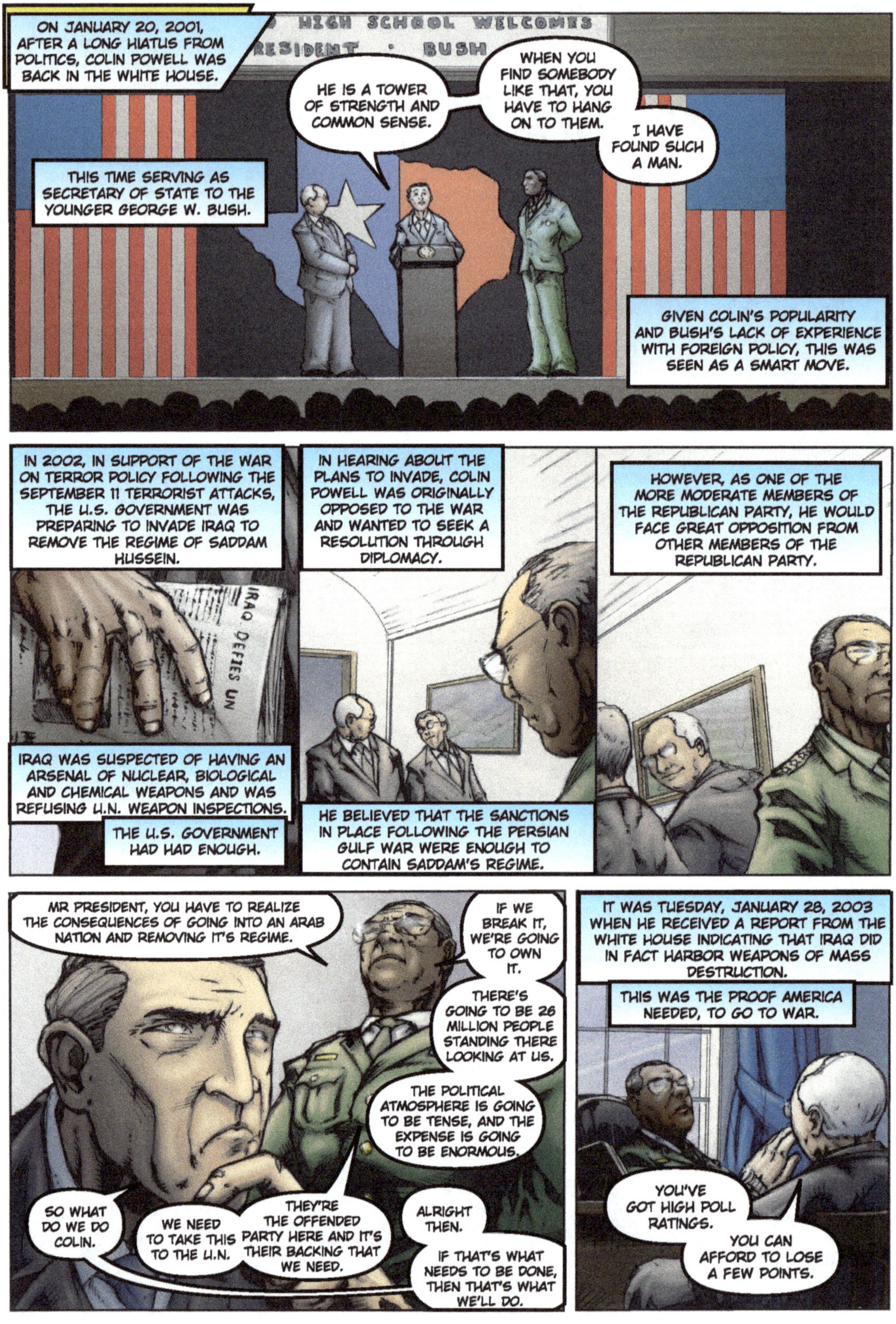
ON JANUARY 20, 2001, AFTER A LONG HIATUS FROM POLITICS, COLIN POWELL WAS BACK IN THE WHITE HOUSE.
HIGH SCHOOL WELCOMES
RESIDENT · BUSH
HE IS A TOWER OF STRENGTH AND COMMON SENSE.
WHEN YOU FIND SOMEBODY LIKE THAT, YOU HAVE TO HANG ON TO THEM.
I HAVE FOUND SUCH A MAN.
THIS TIME SERVING AS SECRETARY OF STATE TO THE YOUNGER GEORGE W. BUSH.
GIVEN COLIN'S POPULARITY AND BUSH'S LACK OF EXPERIENCE WITH FOREIGN POLICY, THIS WAS SEEN AS A SMART MOVE.
IN 2002, IN SUPPORT OF THE WAR ON TERROR POLICY FOLLOWING THE SEPTEMBER 11 TERRORIST ATTACKS, THE U.S. GOVERNMENT WAS PREPARING TO INVADE IRAQ TO REMOVE THE REGIME OF SADDAM HUSSEIN.
IRAQ DEFIES UN
IRAQ WAS SUSPECTED OF HAVING AN ARSENAL OF NUCLEAR, BIOLOGICAL AND CHEMICAL WEAPONS AND WAS REFUSING U.N. WEAPON INSPECTIONS.
THE U.S. GOVERNMENT HAD HAD ENOUGH.
IN HEARING ABOUT THE PLANS TO INVADE, COLIN POWELL WAS ORIGINALLY OPPOSED TO THE WAR AND WANTED TO SEEK A RESOLUTION THROUGH DIPLOMACY.
HE BELIEVED THAT THE SANCTIONS IN PLACE FOLLOWING THE PERSIAN GULF WAR WERE ENOUGH TO CONTAIN SADDAM'S REGIME.
HOWEVER, AS ONE OF THE MORE MODERATE MEMBERS OF THE REPUBLICAN PARTY, HE WOULD FACE GREAT OPPOSITION FROM OTHER MEMBERS OF THE REPUBLICAN PARTY.
MR PRESIDENT, YOU HAVE TO REALIZE THE CONSEQUENCES OF GOING INTO AN ARAB NATION AND REMOVING IT'S REGIME.
IF WE BREAK IT, WE'RE GOING TO OWN IT.
THERE'S GOING TO BE 26 MILLION PEOPLE STANDING THERE LOOKING AT US.
THE POLITICAL ATMOSPHERE IS GOING TO BE TENSE, AND THE EXPENSE IS GOING TO BE ENORMOUS.
SO WHAT DO WE DO COLIN.
WE NEED TO TAKE THIS TO THE U.N.
THEY'RE THE OFFENDED PARTY HERE AND IT'S THEIR BACKING THAT WE NEED.
ALRIGHT THEN.
IF THAT'S WHAT NEEDS TO BE DONE, THEN THAT'S WHAT WE'LL DO.
IT WAS TUESDAY, JANUARY 28, 2003 WHEN HE RECEIVED A REPORT FROM THE WHITE HOUSE INDICATING THAT IRAQ DID IN FACT HARBOR WEAPONS OF MASS DESTRUCTION.
THIS WAS THE PROOF AMERICA NEEDED, TO GO TO WAR.
YOU'VE GOT HIGH POLL RATINGS.
YOU CAN AFFORD TO LOSE A FEW POINTS.

FEBRUARY 5, 2003
COLIN DELIVERED THE SPEECH THAT WOULD TURN HIS CAREER UPSIDE DOWN.
MY COLLEAGUES, OVER THREE MONTHS AGO THIS COUNCIL RECOGNIZED THAT IRAQ CONTINUED TO POSE A THREAT TO INTERNATIONAL PEACE AND SECURITY...
....AND HAT IRAQ HAD BEEN AND REMAINED IN MATERIAL BREACH OF ITS DISARMAMENT OBLIGATIONS.
TODAY IRAQ STILL POSES A THREAT AND IRAQ STILL REMAINS IN MATERIAL BREACH.
INDEED, BY ITS FAILURE TO SEIZE ON ITS ONE LAST OPPORTUNITY TO COME CLEAN AND DISARM...
...IRAQ HAS PUT ITSELF IN DEEPER MATERIAL BREACH AND CLOSER TO THE DAY WHEN IT WILL FACE SERIOUS CONSEQUENCES FOR ITS CONTINUED DEFIANCE OF THIS COUNCIL.
UNITED STATES
AMID MASS WORLDWIDE PROTESTS, THE UN BACKED FORCES INVADED IRAQ A MONTH LATER.
LEAVE IRAQ
NO MORE WAR
THE IRAQ INVASION WAS INITIALLY A SUCCESS -
- BUT IT WAS THE AFTERMATH AND CIVIL WAR THAT FOLLOWED WHICH WOULD MAR COLIN'S CAREER.
THE DOCUMENT HE HAD PRESENTED TO THE UN COUNCILS TO GARNER SUPPORT OF THE INVASION WAS FOUND TO BE FALSE.
SOME BELIEVED POWELL HAD BEEN FOOLED BY HIS OWN PARTY, A VICTIM OF HIS CONFLICT WITH CERTAIN INDIVIDUALS IDEOLOGIES.
THE ONCE GREAT AMERICAN HERO WOULD NOW HAVE HIS CREDIBILITY QUESTIONED.
FOLLOWING THE 2004 REELECTION OF PRESIDENT BUSH INTO HIS SECOND TERM, POWELL RECEIVED AT PHONE CALL AT HIS OFFICE.
THE PRESIDENT WOULD LIKE TO MAKE A CHANGE.
IT WAS A BITTER END TO HIS TERM AS SECRETARY OF STATE.

OPRAH
WINFREY

EASTER SUNDAY.
1957.
SHE SURE IS SOME'N SPECIAL.
HATTIE MAE, THAT CHILD IS GIFTED.
JESUS ROSE ON EASTER DAY. HALELU, HALELU, ALL THE ANGELS DID PROCLAIM.
THIS CHILD SHO' CAN TALK!
THREE-YEARS-OLD, AND SHE ALREADY READ'N, YOU KNOW THAT?
WRITE'N TOO. GIRL, THAT CHILD IS GOING SOMEWHERE.
BORN TO UNWED PARENTS IN A TIME WHEN JOBS WERE SCARCE AND SINGLE MOTHERS WERE ILL EQUIPPED, THIS BEAUTIFUL YOUNG CHILD WILL GROW UP ENDURING UNIMAGINABLE ABUSES FROM THOSE CLOSEST TO HER AND RISE THROUGH IT ALL TO BECOME ONE OF THE WORLD'S MOST INFLUENTIAL VOICES.
HER NAME IS OPRAH GAIL WINFREY AND HER'S IS A STORY WORTH TELLING.
BUT, BEFORE WE GET INTO THAT, LET'S GET SOMETHING OUT OF THE WAY:

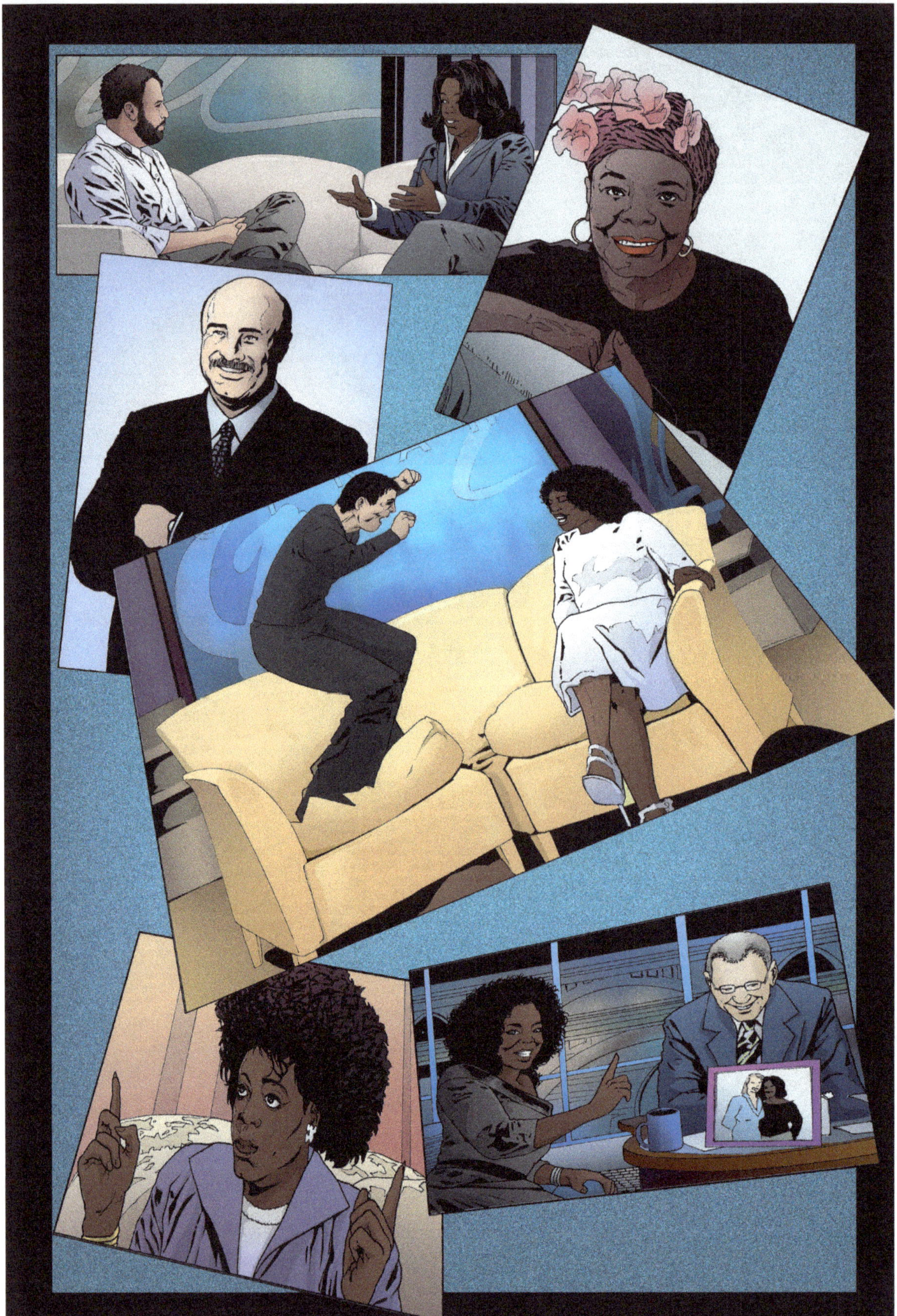

LEFT TO BE RAISED BY HER GRANDPARENTS ON THEIR SMALL FARM IN KOSCIUSKO, MISSISSIPPI, OPRAH'S MOTHER, VERNITA LEE, MOVED TO MILWAUKEE TO FIND WORK.

WITH SO FEW FRIENDS, SHE GAVE THE FARM ANIMALS NAMES, CREATING HER FIRST AUDIENCE.
UNTO THOSE THINGS WHICH ARE BEFORE, I PRESS TOWARD THE MARK FOR THE PRIZE OF THE HIGH CALLING...
OPRAH!
WHEN SHE WAS OLD ENOUGH TO HELP OUT, HER MAIN CHORES WERE FEEDING THE CHICKENS AND CARRYING WATER FROM THE WELL 100 YARDS AWAY TO THE HOUSE.
YOU BEEN PLAYIN' IN THAT WATER, GIRL?
NO, MAMMA.
YOU BEST GET IN HERE, LESS'N YOU WANT ANOTHER WHOOP'N!
HER GRANDMOTHER, WHOM SHE CALLED 'MAMMA', WAS A STERN DISCIPLINARIAN AND QUICK WITH THE SWITCH IN THE DAYS BEFORE 'CHILD ABUSE' WAS A HOUSEHOLD PHRASE.

OPRAH WAS BEATEN ALMOST DAILY.
FOR HER 'OWN GOOD'.
GOD BLESSES YOU BETTER WHEN YOU PRAY ON YOUR KNEES.
SHE PRAYED FOR BOUNCIN' CURLS LIKE SHIRLEY TEMPLE.
AND SHE WISHED FOR A FAMILY LIKE IN 'LEAVE IT TO BEAVER'
WHERE THE KIDS WERE TALKED TO INSTEAD OF BEATEN.

1960.
HAVING SECURED A JOB AS A MAID MAKING $50 PER WEEK, VERNITA LEE SENT FOR OPRAH.
THE FAST-PACED LIFESTYLE OF THE BIG CITY WAS NOT THE ONLY THING OPRAH WOULD HAVE TO ADJUST TO:
SHE HAD A NEW BABY SISTER.
HER MOTHER ADORED AND DOTED ON HER NEW LIGHTER-SKINNED HALF SISTER. OPRAH WAS MADE TO FEEL UGLY FROM THE CONSTANT COMPARISONS.
COME ON, BABY, THIS GONNA BE FUN, Y'KNOW?
OH, ISN'T YOUR LITTLE SISTER THE PRETTIEST THING? WHY DON'T YOU COME HELP ME CHANGE HER.
ALL OF OPRAH'S OBVIOUS TALENTS AND INTELLIGENCE WOULD COUNT FOR NOTHING TO VERNITA LEE, WHO SAW HER AS A SHOW-OFF FOR HER AVID READING.
BUT TAKING CARE OF THE TWO GIRLS IN THE ONE-ROOM APARTMENT EVENTUALLY BECAME TOO MUCH FOR VERNITA LEE.
HATTIE MAE REFUSING TO TAKE OPRAH BACK ON THE FARM, VERNITA AGREED TO LET OPRAH GO TO NASHVILLE TO LIVE WITH HER FATHER.

HAVING HAD A RECENT MISCARRIAGE AND WARNED BY THEIR DOCTOR THAT IT MIGHT BE DANGEROUS TO TRY AGAIN, VERNON AND ZELMA WELCOMED OPRAH INTO THEIR HOME WITH OPEN ARMS.
HER STEPMOTHER ZELMA EXPECTED OPRAH TO READ A BOOK EACH WEEK ON WHICH SHE HAD TO WRITE A REPORT. IN ADDITION, SHE WAS REQUIRED TO ADD A SET NUMBER OF NEW WORDS TO HER VOCABULARY WEEKLY.
IN HER FATHER'S HOME, OPRAH WAS STARTING TO GET THE STRUCTURE AND ENCOURAGEMENT VERNITA WAS UNABLE TO GIVE.
WHILE VISITING HER MOTHER THE FOLLOWING SUMMER, VERNITA DECIDED NOT TO LET OPRAH GO BACK WITH HER FATHER TO NASHVILLE. SHE TOLD OPRAH THAT THE FATHER OF HER *NEW BABY* BROTHER WAS GOING TO MARRY HER AND MOVE THEM ALL INTO A HOUSE OF THEIR OWN.
VERNON KNEW THAT OPRAH WAS GOING RIGHT BACK INTO THE SAME SITUATION FROM WHICH HE RESCUED HIS DAUGHTER.
BUT WITHOUT LEGAL CUSTODY, THERE WAS NOTHING HE COULD DO

VERNITA, HER BOYFRIEND, OPRAH, AND HER TWO SIBLINGS, MOVED INTO A CRAMPED TWO-BEDROOM APARTMENT WHERE MANY OTHER FAMILY MEMBERS AND FRIENDS DRIFTED IN AND OUT.
"THE CAGED BIRD SINGS WITH A FEARFUL TRILL."
"OF THINGS UNKNOWN BUT LONGED FOR STILL."
"AND HIS TUNE IS HEARD ON THE DISTANT HILL."
"FOR THE CAGED BIRD SINGS OF FREEDOM." - MAYA ANGELOU
AT THE AGE OF NINE, OPRAH WAS RAPED BY A COUSIN WHO BABYSAT HER OFTEN.
LIKE SO MANY OTHER YOUNG WOMEN, SHE REMAINED SILENT, THINKING IT WAS SOMEHOW HER FAULT.
MANY OTHER MEN, FRIENDS AND FAMILY MEMBERS ALIKE, MOLESTED AND RAPED HER WHILE LIVING AT HER MOTHER'S APARTMENT. SHE WAS PASSED AROUND AMONGST THEM.

1968.
LINCOLN HIGH SCHOOL, MILWAUKEE, WI.
A TEACHER BY THE NAME OF GENE ABRAMS RECOGNIZED THE POTENTIAL IN OPRAH AND MADE IT HIS MISSION TO GET HER OUT OF THE ROUGH ENVIRONMENT OF LINCOLN.
SHE WAS RECOMMENDED FOR 'UPWARD BOUND', A SCHOLARSHIP PROGRAM THAT PLACED MINORITIES INTO PRIVATE ALL-WHITE HIGH SCHOOLS.
NICOLET HIGH SCHOOL
AS THE ONLY BLACK STUDENT AT NICOLET HIGH SCHOOL, OPRAH BECAME INSTANTLY POPULAR. SHE WAS A CURIOSITY AND WAS OFTEN INVITED TO STUDENT'S HOMES.
AS MUCH AS SHE EXCELLED AT SCHOOL, OPRAH RAN WILD AT HOME.
DESPERATE FOR THE LOVE OF A MOTHER WHO WAS SELF-ABSORBED, OPRAH SOUGHT ATTENTION WHEREVER SHE COULD GET IT.

IT TOOK TWENTY MILES AND THREE BUSES TO GET TO HER NEW SCHOOL EVERY DAY.
SHE FELT LIKE CINDERELLA RETURNING HOME FROM THE CASTLE EVERY NIGHT.
THE VISITS TO THE HOMES OF HER CLASSMATES OPENED HER EYES TO JUST HOW DIFFERENT HER LIFE WAS.
SHE WAS STARTING TO SEE JUST HOW DIFFERENT *SHE* WAS.
AND YOU BETTER NOT *ACCIDENTALLY* FALL DOWN AND BREAK THOSE, NEITHER! GOOD MONEY BOUGHT THOSE GLASSES AND I CAN'T AFFORD TO BUY YOU NO NEW ONES JUST 'CAUSE YOU WANNA LOOK 'HIP' FOR YOUR LITTLE FRIENDS.
SO... UGLY.

I DON'T SEE ANYTHING...
...PHYSICALLY WRONG AT ALL, BUT SHE SAYS THAT SHE CAN'T REMEMBER ANYTHING THAT HAPPENED.
SAYS SHE HAS 'AMNESIA'.
LUCKILY, NOTHING SEEMS TO BE MISSING IN YOUR APARTMENT.
IN FACT, THE ONLY THING EVEN DAMAGED WAS YOUR DAUGHTER'S GLASSES.
HER... GLASSES?
YEAH, SMASHED TO BITS.
VERNITA LEE'S 'DO AS I SAY AND NOT AS I DO' STRATEGY HAD ULTIMATELY FAILED.
OPRAH'S UNRULY AND PROMISCUOUS WAYS WERE PROBLEMS THAT VERNITA WASN'T PREPARED TO HANDLE.
SHE SAW ONLY ONE OPTION:
OFFICERS? COULD YOU PLEASE GIVE ME A MINUTE ALONE?
WITH MY... DAUGHTER?
VERNON? COME GET YOUR DAUGHTER.

BACK AT HER FATHER'S HOUSE, VERNON HAD HIS WORK CUT OUT FOR HIM.
LISTEN, GIRL, IF I TELL YOU A MOSQUITO CAN PULL A WAGON, DON'T ASK ME NO QUESTIONS. JUST HITCH HIM UP.
THE WAY I SEE IT, THERE ARE THREE KINDS OF PEOPLE IN THE WORLD:
THE FIRST MAKES THINGS HAPPEN.
THE SECOND WATCHES THINGS HAPPEN.
AND THE THIRD, WELL, THE THIRD'S NOT QUITE SURE WHAT'S HAPPENING.
WHAT KIND OF PERSON DO YOU WANT TO BE?
Life of Sojourner Tr
Ain't I a Woman
NARRATI
SOJOURNER TRUTH
OPRAH'S STEPMOTHER, ZELMA, BROUGHT HER TO THE LIBRARY EVERY TWO WEEKS TO PICK FIVE BOOKS ON WHICH SHE HAD TO DO REPORTS.
OPRAH'S NEED FOR LOVE AND ATTENTION WAS CHANNELED IN A NEW DIRECTION.
HER LIFE STARTED TO TURN AROUND.

The Mighty 147
WVOL
WHILE SHE WAS A SENIOR IN HIGH SCHOOL, JOHN HEIDELBERG, A DISC JOCKEY AT WVOL RADIO, NOTICED OPRAH'S RESONANT AND ARTICULATE VOICE AND CONVINCED HER TO MAKE A DEMO TAPE.
SHE WAS HIRED TO DO NEWS REPORTS ON THE WEEKENDS AND AFTER SCHOOL FOR $100 PER WEEK.
OPRAH GRADUATED FROM EAST NASHVILLE HIGH SCHOOL WHERE SHE WAS VOTED 'MOST POPULAR GIRL'.
SHE WENT ON TO ATTEND TENNESSEE STATE UNIVERSITY WHERE SHE MAJORED IN SPEECH AND DRAMA.
OPRAH SEIZED THE OPPORTUNITY TO ENTER A LOCAL BEAUTY PAGEANT AND WENT ON TO WIN SEVERAL TITLES, INCLUDING: MISS FIRE PREVENTION, MISS BLACK NASHVILLE, AND MISS BLACK TENNESSEE.
1973.
SHE WAS HIRED BY WTVF-TV AND, AT 19, BECAME THE YOUNGEST PERSON AND THE FIRST AFRICAN AMERICAN TO ANCHOR THE NEWS IN NASHVILLE.

1976.
VERNON AND ZELMA PUT HER ON THE RIGHT PATH, BUT IT WAS TIME FOR OPRAH TO BECOME INDEPENDENT.
HIRED BY WJZ-TV, OPRAH MOVED TO BALTIMORE TO CO-HOST THE 6 O'CLOCK NEWS.
IT WAS AT WJZ-TV THAT OPRAH MET HER BEST FRIEND GAYLE KING, AN INTERN AT THE TIME.
SEEN AS TOO *EMOTIONAL* TO ANCHOR THE NEWS, OPRAH WAS 'DEMOTED' TO CO-HOST A DAYTIME TALK SHOW UNTIL HER CONTRACT RAN OUT.
ON *'PEOPLE ARE TALKING'*, SHE AND HER NEW CO-HOST RICHARD SHER'S ON-AIR CHEMISTRY LED THE SHOW TO BEAT OUT THE PHIL DONAHUE SHOW IN LOCAL MARKETS.
OPRAH FELT LIKE SHE FINALLY FOUND WHAT SHE WAS MEANT TO DO. BUT SHE KNEW THAT SHE COULDN'T REALLY BE HERSELF AS A CO-HOST.
WHEN SHE HEARD THAT A SHOW IN CHICAGO WAS LOOKING FOR A HOST, OPRAH SEIZED THE OPPORTUNITY AND BECAME OBSESSED WITH GETTING THE JOB.

SHE WAS HIRED AS THE NEW HOST OF 'A.M. CHICAGO'.
IN LESS THAN A MONTH, IT BECAME THE NUMBER ONE TALK SHOW IN THE CHICAGO MARKET.
OPRAH HAD A SENSE THAT SHE HAD COME 'HOME'.
1985.
THE SHOW ENJOYED SUCH SUCCESS, THAT IT WAS RENAMED:
I'M OPRAH WINFREY AND WELCOME TO THE *FIRST NATIONAL OPRAH WINFREY SHOW!*

SHE IS A TELEVISION PIONEER, AN ACTRESS AND PRODUCER.
SHE IS A MULTI-FACETED ENTREPRENEUR WHO HAS CHANNELED HER ENORMOUS WEALTH INTO A LIFE OF INCREDIBLE PHILANTHROPY.
SHE INITIATED THE *NATIONAL CHILD PROTECTION ACT,* SIGNED INTO LAW BY PRESIDENT BILL CLINTON.
SHE BUILT THE LEADERSHIP ACADEMY FOR GIRLS IN SOUTH AFRICA.
OPRAH'S ANGEL NETWORK HAS RAISED OVER $80 MILLION FOR GRANTS AND CHARITABLE PROJECTS AROUND THE WORLD.
BUT TO ME, THIS IS THE STORY OF THE GIRL WHO *BECAME* OPRAH WINFREY.

"You may encounter many defeats, but you must not be defeated."
IT'S A STORY ABOUT A LITTLE GIRL WHO WAS BEATEN BUT NEVER BROKEN.
"I AM WHAT I AM BECAUSE OF MY GRANDMOTHER. MY STRENGTH. MY SENSE OF REASONING, EVERYTHING. ALL THAT WAS SET BY THE TIME I WAS SIX."
"In fact, it may be necessary to encounter the defeats...
IT'S ABOUT SOMEONE WHO WAS ABLE TO TURN HER WOUNDS INTO WISDOM.
"...so you can know who you are, what you can rise from..."
"HER WAY OF SHOWING LOVE TO ME WAS GETTING OUT AND GOING TO WORK EVERY DAY, PUTTING CLOTHES ON MY BACK AND HAVING FOOD ON THE TABLE. AT THAT TIME I DIDN'T UNDERSTAND IT."
"How you can still come out of it."
- Maya Angelou
IT'S ABOUT SALVATION AND SECOND CHANCES AND ABOUT SEIZING OPPORTUNITIES.
"WHEN MY FATHER TOOK ME, IT CHANGED THE COURSE OF MY LIFE. HE SAVED ME."
"IT IS BECAUSE OF HIM THAT I AM WHERE I AM TODAY."
-OPRAH WINFREY

The Color Purple
OPRAH WINFREY
OPRAH WINFREY DANNY GLOVER
"Two Thumbs Up!"
"One Of The Most Powerful Films Of The Year!"
BELOVED
IT'S ABOUT ACHIEVING YOUR DREAMS BUT NOT STOPPING THERE.
IT'S ABOUT FIGHTING FOR WHAT YOU BELIEVE IN.
Book OPRAH'S Club
AND LEAVING THE WORLD A BETTER PLACE THAN YOU FOUND IT.
IT'S ABOUT LEADING BY EXAMPLE.
AND WALKING THE TALK.

LADIES AND GENTLEMEN, THE LIFETIME ACHIEVEMENT AWARD TO...
OPRAH WINFREY!
I WOULD LIKE TO THANK EVERYBODY WHO HAS NURTURED ME, WHO HAS STOOD IN THE GAP FOR ME.
"WE ARE ALL BEACONS OF LIGHT FOR EACH OTHER."
IT'S ABOUT GREAT ACHIEVEMENT WITH NO END IN SIGHT.

OPRAH!
IT'S OPRAH!
OPRAH!
OPRAH!
HARPO STUDIOS
THE OPRAH WINFREY SHOW
HELLO! HELLO! WELCOME TO THE SHOW!
"BREATHE."
"LET GO."

"AND REMIND YOURSELF THAT THIS VERY MOMENT..."
IT'S ABOUT NEVER FORGETTING WHERE YOU CAME FROM.
"IS THE ONLY ONE YOU KNOW YOU HAVE FOR SURE."
AND NEVER LOSING WHO YOU ARE.

GOD, USE ME. USE ME. USE THIS LIFE. I DON'T KNOW WHAT THE FUTURE HOLDS FOR ME BUT I KNOW THAT THERE IS A VISION FOR MY LIFE THAT IS GREATER THAN MY IMAGINATION CAN HOLD.
"USE ME. USE ME. WHAT WOULD YOU HAVE ME TO DO?"
I AM NOT HERE TO TELL YOU WHAT TO THINK.
I AM HERE TO TELL YOU TO THINK.
CHANGE
WE CAN BELIEVE IN
"FOR EVERYONE OF US THAT SUCCEEDS, IT'S BECAUSE THERE'S SOMEBODY THERE TO SHOW YOU THE WAY OUT."
-OPRAH WINFREY

BIBLIOGRAPHIES

BARACK OBAMA

BOOKS

Dreams from my Father by Barack Obama. 1995, 2004, Three Rivers Press.
The Audacity of Hope by Barack Obama. 2006, Three Rivers Press.
Barack Obama: Presidential Collector's Vault by Avery Krut. 2009, Whitman Publishing.
Rolling Stone Commemorative Edition: Barack Obama. 2008.
'08: A Graphic Diary of the Campaign Trail by Michael Crowley and Dan Goldman. 2009. Three Rivers Press.

WEBSITES

http://en.wikipedia.org/wiki/Loving_v._Virginia
http://www.chicagomag.com/Chicago-Magazine/January-1993/Vote-of-Confidence/
http://www.associatedcontent.com/article/357871/illinois_governors_office_no_stranger.html
http://www.youtube.com/watch?v=I7f0rH1fxkw&feature=related
http://www.washingtonpost.com/wp-srv/politics/documents/transcript_david_plouffe_011209.html/
http://www.desmoinesregister.com/apps/pbcs.dll/article?AID=/20080101/NEWS09/301010015/-1/iowapoll07
http://www.youtube.com/watch?v=2fdaWzVFS4c
http://www.youtube.com/watch?v=c9-1JmTQFoc
http://en.wikipedia.org/wiki/Shepard_Fairey
http://en.wikipedia.org/wiki/John_McCain
http://edition.cnn.com/2008/POLITICS/05/17/obama.mccain.flap/index.html
http://blogs.suntimes.com/sweet/2008/11/bill_ayers_on_abcs_good_mornin.html
http://en.wikipedia.org/wiki/Ann_Nixon_Cooper
http://www.nytimes.com/2008/11/04/us/politics/04text-mccain.html
http://www.whitehouse.gov/blog/inaugural-address/

CONDOLEEZZA RICE

BOOKS

Condoleezza Rice: An American Life. Elisabeth Bumiller. Random House Books, 2009
Bush at War. Bob Woodward. Simon & Schuster, 2002.
Plan of Attack. Bob Woodward. Simon & Schuster, 2004.
State of Denial: Bush at War, Part III. Bob Woodward. Simon & Schuster, 2006.
Twice As Good: Condoleezza Rice and Her Path to Power. Marcus Mabry. Modern Times, 2007.

WEBSITES

http://www.huffingtonpost.com/2009/03/25/condoleezza-rice-on-jay-l_n_178985.html
http://www.users.globalnet.co.uk/~liden/zen_songs.html
http://en.wikipedia.org/wiki/Vulcan_statue
http://www.time.com/time/magazine/article/0,9171,986714,00.html
http://www.africanaonline.com/civil_rights_birmingham.htm
http://www.carruthersrealestate.com/news_021108.html
http://en.wikipedia.org/wiki/16th_Street_Baptist_Church_bombing
http://en.wikipedia.org/wiki/Millie_(dog)
http://www.youtube.com/watch?v=C0f2dHJ6A18
http://www.cbsnews.com/video/watch/?id=1999157n
http://edition.cnn.com/2004/ALLPOLITICS/04/08/rice.transcript/
http://www.mideastweb.org/iraqtimeline.htm
http://www.nytimes.com/2003/01/23/opinion/23RICE.html
http://www.tbrnews.org/Archives/a691.htm
http://historymike.blogspot.com/2006/07/condi-to-play-piano-at-forum-i-keep.html

COLIN POWELL

BOOKS

My American Journey - by Colin Powell 1995
Soldier:The Life of Collin Powell - by Karen DeYoung 2006
Colin Powell Biography - by Reggie Finlayson - Lerner Publications (August 2003)

WEBSITES

http://www.washingtonpost.com/wp-dyn/content/article/2006/09/27/AR2006092700106.html
http://en.wikipedia.org/wiki/Colin_Powell
http://www.citizensmedal.com/ColinPowell.htm
http://www.achievement.org/autodoc/page/pow0int-1
http://www.achievement.org/autodoc/page/pow0bio-1
http://www.achievement.org/autodoc/page/pow0gal-1
http://community.seattletimes.nwsource.com/archive/?date=19910210&slug=1265511
http://www.flickr.com/photos/kencta/225227236/
http://www.nydailynews.com/archives/news/1995/10/08/1995-10-08_colin_powell_s_new_york__byg.html
http://maps.google.com.au/maps?f=d&source=s_d&saddr=1007+tiffany+st+bronx&daddr=952+kelly+st+bronx&hl=en&geocode=&mra=ls&sll=40.81837,-73.89427&sspn=0.00313,0.006974&ie=UTF8&ll=40.82149,-73.894891&spn=0.00626,0.013947&t=h&z=17
http://www.grandmagazine.com/articl e.asp?id=60
http://www.cnn.com/ALLPOLITICS/1996/news/9604/11/alma/index.shtml
http://en.wikipedia.org/wiki/Birmingham_campaign
http://en.wikipedia.org/wiki/Mikhail_Gorbachev
http://en.wikipedia.org/wiki/Gulf_War
http://edition.cnn.com/2003/US/02/05/sprj.irq.powell.transcript.10/index.html
http://www.aaregistry.com/african_american_history/637/The_first_African_American_secretary_of_state_Colin_Powell
http://www.washingtonpost.com/wp-srv/onpolitics/elections/gop2000guide/powellpost.htm

OPRAH WINFREY

DVDS

Oprah: Unauthorized – Crystal Ent. And Medialink Ent.
Finding Oprah's Roots, Finding Your Own – PBS Paramount

BOOKS

Oprah Winfrey: The Real Story – George Mair
Oprah Winfrey Speaks: Insights from the World's Most Influential Voice – Janet Lowe
Oprah! – Robert Waldron

WEBSITES

www.Oprah.com
http://www.youtube.com/watch?v=JaaPTUbaH_s
http://www.youtube.com/watch?v=lwhw0ugynl8
http://www.youtube.com/watch?v=zg3T96fUZro

PERSONAL THANKS TO

John Heidelberg, WVOL Radio
Vernon Winfrey

BLUEWATER COMICS

★ BLACK ★ HISTORY ★

LEADERS

Barack Obama

Writer: Chris Ward
Art: Azim Akberali
Letters: Jaymes Reed

Condoleezza Rice

Writer: Chris Ward
Pencils & Inks: Dave MacNeil
Colors: Osmarco Valladao
Letters: Jaymes Reed

Colin Powell

Writer: Wey-Yuih Loh
Pencils: M. Scott Woodward
Colors: Kirtsy Swan
Letters: Wilson Ramos Jr.

Oprah Winfrey

Writer and Pencils: Joshua LaBello
Colors: Michelle Davies
Letters: Wilson Ramos Jr.

Pin-ups

Vinnie Tartamella & Patricio Carbajal

Cover: Patricio Carbajal

Patrick Foster
Logo Design

Chad Jones
Production

Darren G. Davis
Publisher

Jason Schultz
Vice President

Lisa K. Brause
Entertainment Manager

Lisa Battan
Marketing Director

Janda Tithia
Coordinator

Scott Davis
Media Manager

Joshua LaBello
Creative Services

Vonnie Harris
New Business

Adam Ellis
Coordinator

BLUEWATER COMICS

www.bluewaterprod.com

CPSIA information can be obtained
at www.ICGtesting.com
Printed in the USA
LVHW061533300119
605809LV00005B/68/P

9 781616 239237